THE LIVING
LEGEND OF
ST PATRICK

THE LIVING LEGEND OF ST PATRICK

Alannah Hopkin

GRAFTON BOOKS
A Division of the Collins Publishing Group

LONDON GLASGOW
TORONTO SYDNEY AUCKLAND

Grafton Books
A Division of the Collins Publishing Group
8 Grafton Street, London W1X 3LA

Published by Grafton Books 1989

British Library Cataloguing in Publication Data

Hopkin, Alannah
  The living legend of St Patrick.
  1. Christian church. Patrick, Saint
  I. Title
  270.2′092′4

ISBN 0-246-13099-7

Typeset by Ace Filmsetting Ltd, Frome, Somerset
Printed in Great Britain by Hartnolls Ltd, Bodmin

CONTENTS

ACKNOWLEDGEMENTS

I would like to thank the Librarians and staff of the National Library, Dublin; the Boole Library, University College, Cork; and the London Library for their help. Also the staff of the Linenhall Library, Belfast, the Catholic Central Library, London, and the Central Catholic Library, Dublin. Special thanks to Sean Phillips, the Librarian of University College, Dublin.

Thanks to Tim Magennis of the Irish Tourist Board for practical and enthusiastic advice, and to Ian Hill and his staff at the Northern Ireland Tourist Board, Belfast, for hospitality and helpful suggestions.

I am particularly grateful to those academics and professional historians who had the time and the patience to discuss Saint Patrick with me:

F. X. Martin, Professor of Medieval History, University College, Dublin; Charles Doherty, Lecturer in Early Irish History, University College, Dublin; Professor R. P. C. Hanson; Richard Sharpe M.A., Assistant Editor of the *Dictionary of Medieval Latin from British Sources*; A. J. R. Harvey M.A. Ph.D., Editorial Secretary of the *Dictionary of Medieval Latin from Celtic Sources*; Kevin T. McEneaney of the American Irish Historical Society; Dr Seamus Ó Cathain, Archivist of the Department of Folklore, University College, Dublin; Dáithi Ó hÓgaín, Lecturer in Folklore, University College, Dublin; D. C. Rose B.A.; Brian Murphy M.A., Ph.D.; Lawrence Flynn; Albert W. K. Colmer.

Thanks also to Mrs Eva Bieler, Revd Monsignor Gerard McSorley, Canon Joseph Maguire, P. P. Downpatrick; Edward J. Boyle Jr. of New Orleans; Benedict A. Gillespie of Puerto Rico; John J. Concannon of New York; 'Ragtime' Bob Darch; the Librarian of the *Irish Times*; Conleth Duffy of the Westport

Archaeological Society; Margaret Foley of Tramore; Mary E. Pollard of Armagh; Aidan Brady, Director of the National Botanic Gardens, Glasnevin; Paddy Derevan and Peter Harbison of the Irish Tourist Board; Alf O'Brien of U.C.C.; Professor Sean Lucy; Brian Fallon; the late Ian Fordyce; Gay Byrne, the producers of the Gay Byrne Show and the many listeners who wrote to me about Saint Patrick; and all the kind people I met on my travels.

Special thanks to Father Patrick D. Dundon of the Irish Missionary Union, and to Derek Mahon for many helpful suggestions.

I am greatly indebted to those who read the first draft: Charles Davidson, whose detailed comments were greatly appreciated; Desmond O'Grady for invaluable advice and encouragement; and Diana Gishing for tactful suggestions on matters of style.

Very special thanks are due to my agent, Reg Davis-Poynter; to Betty Palmer; and to Ellen Beardsley who word-processed the first draft and its corrections with astounding speed and accuracy.

Finally, thanks to my family and friends who provoked many fruitful discussions; to my parents; and to Aidan.

Alannah Hopkin
Kinsale, Co. Cork, 1988

INTRODUCTION

Many volumes have been written about Saint Patrick and his life. This book is more concerned with the images of Saint Patrick held in different ages, and their significance, than with the saint himself.

Saint Patrick has become associated with a particular national stereotype which many Irish people detest. Garrulity, sentimental religiosity, quaintness, deviousness combined with naïvety – its very name is derived from the saint himself: Paddywhackery. Rejection of this stereotype in modern Ireland has been accompanied by a decline in interest in Saint Patrick, which has probably never been at a lower ebb. This is, however, in a way a positive development, as it also represents the rejection of the many bogus traditions and superstitions that have become associated with the saint during the long history of his cult.

Saint Patrick did indeed exist, but the scant facts available about his life did not become common knowledge until the twentieth century. Many people still confuse the Saint Patrick of legend with the very different historical figure. Early Irish society rewrote Saint Patrick's life as that of a secular hero. In medieval times his life was rewritten again, this time to conform to the continental idea of sainthood. The modern image of Saint Patrick started to emerge in the late eighteenth century, when he was adopted as a symbol of the nationalist movement. The various ways in which he has been presented over the centuries must be understood if the historical Saint Patrick and his legacy are to be disassociated from Paddywhackery.

Saint Patrick does not only belong to the Irish who have stayed at home. The Irish abroad and those of Irish descent around the world have made 17 March an international occasion on which the Irish and their friends celebrate his name. The way in which they do so is often criticized, particularly for its emphasis on alcohol, but even this apparently irrelevant association has a long history. In New York millions of people watch a highly organized parade lasting some six hours make its way down Fifth Avenue. In San Antonio, Texas, they dye the river green. Parades are held as far afield as Alaska, Puerto Rico, Montreal and Sydney, Australia, celebrating a kind of Irishness that would hardly be recognized in Ireland itself, and yet originated there.

The search for Saint Patrick is not only a geographical one, although I have described many of the sites and pilgrimages in Ireland associated with the saint. It is also a historical search, which travels down the centuries through the social, cultural, intellectual and spiritual life of the Irish people. It begins by outlining the little that is known about the historical Saint Patrick, a Romano-British bishop of the fifth century.

1

EGO PATRICIUS

Ego Patricius peccator rusticissimus et minimus omnium fidelium et contemptibilis sum apud plurimos.

I am Patrick, a sinner, most unlearned, the least of all the faithful, and utterly despised by many.

So begins the *Confession* of Patricius. There is no doubt as to its authenticity. Over the years scholars have disputed just about every aspect of the story of Saint Patrick, but no one has ever credibly argued that his *Confession* was faked. It is too clumsy, too vague and too idiosyncratic to be the the work of a forger.

The difference between the Saint Patrick of legend and the author of the *Confession* is so great that Saint Patrick will be referred to as Patricius throughout this chapter. It is hoped that this device will help to extricate the historical man from the accretions of legend.

Patricius wrote, or perhaps dictated, the *Confession* in Latin when he was an old man. The other surviving piece of writing by Patricius is his *Letter to Coroticus* and in this he tells us in no uncertain terms: 'With my own hands have I written and composed these words.' Taken together, the two texts provide us with a tantalizing picture of the man Patricius. His firm, straightforward character lives in his words. There can be no doubt of his sincerity, his humility and his steadfastness. But, as one of those scholars who has dedicated his life to the study of these texts has written: 'We would wish their author were as lucid as he is sincere.'

Patricius's Latin is rough, to put it mildly, and he points out more than once that Latin was not his normal daily language. But it is the very imperfection of his writing, the feeling that he is often fumbling for words, falling back on biblical quotation when all else fails – he uses over 200 of these – and breaking into spontaneous prayer, that brings Patricius so much alive as a man. Augustine, who was writing his *Confession* in Hippo a generation before Patricius wrote his in Ireland, is a far more accomplished rhetorician, but we see Augustine as he wants us to see him. Patricius is incapable of manipulating his readers in that way: the man comes alive in his halting but moving prose.

The *Confession* was written in the middle of the fifth century. That is a remarkable feature in itself: it is the only autobiographical writing surviving from those years in British or Irish annals. A highly individual voice is speaking to us from across the centuries. And, moreover, it is the voice of one of the great saints of the early Christian church, the voice of Patricius himself.

To understand more fully the scholarly excitement generated by the *Confession*, it is important to appreciate just how little is known about Ireland and Britain in the fifth century. Pick up any respectable and serious (as opposed to speculative) work on early Irish history and you will find a veritable Thesaurus of *apologia* for ignorance: 'nothing is known of . . .' '. . . remains impenetrably obscure . . .' 'the scanty surviving evidence suggests . . .' 'hardly less obscure is . . .' '. . . presents an insoluble problem . . .' Professor Gearóid MacNiocaill, who generated all the above phrases in one short chapter of his excellent standard history *Ireland Before the Vikings*, manages to be sure of something at least when he writes: 'The fifth century has been very justly described as a lost century.' Professor Charles Thomas, another authority on the period confirms this: 'The fifth century continues to be the most obscure in our recorded history.' The eminent Irish historian D. A. Binchy, introducing his readers to the period, makes his point by the grand gesture of quoting the closing lines of Matthew Arnold's 'Dover Beach' as a metaphor for the historian faced with the task of making sense of the fifth century:

> And we are here as on a darkling plain
> Swept with confused alarms of struggle and flight
> Where ignorant armies clash by night.

In fact much of the little that we do know about the fifth century is due to the labours of the Patrician scholars, as those who have made a serious study of the life of Saint Patrick are called. That Patricius himself is a major source for the period only adds to the confusion, as there was, until very recently, little external evidence to shed light on his difficult writings. Consequently, up to about twenty years ago, historians of the fifth century in Ireland tended to concentrate largely on the Patrician texts. MacNiocaill is understandably rather scathing about this tendency: 'The problems of Saint Patrick's chronology and mission have largely occupied the attention of the few concerned with early Irish history: not unnaturally, since they afford splendid opportunities for conjecture and abundant scope for the exercise of academic spleen.'

Irish historians refer to the fifth century in positive terms as 'early Christian Ireland'. The British used to call the same period 'the Dark Ages'. In Ireland the fifth century marks the end of the Iron Age, the end of centuries of isolation and the start of the island's entry into the historical world. In Britain the fifth century is a retrograde phase permeated by the darkness which attended the fall of the Roman Empire. It was the age in which the social and political structures of Roman Britain were falling apart.

With the exception of Ireland, it was a time of turmoil for the whole of the western world. Barbarians penetrated even into Italy. In 407, Gaul was invaded by a Vandal horde and Alaric and the Goths sacked Rome. In the middle of the fifth century Attila and the Huns overran what was left of the empire. The Romano-British were at the start of what was to be a losing battle against the Saxons.

Roman Britain did not disappear overnight: it fell apart gradually. Britain had been under Roman occupation for three and a half centuries, and whatever the state of political disarray in the country, in the early fifth century people like Patricius still considered themselves to be Roman Britons, Christians, and intrinsically superior to the marauding barbarians around them.

The full text of the *Confession* and the *Letter to Coroticus* will be found in Appendix I, but, standing as they do alone among British and Irish documents of the time, they cannot simply be left to speak for themselves. A commentary is needed. In order to allow these writings to give a picture of Patricius as he presents himself, I will attempt to steer a non-controversial course through the accumulation of learned commentary on his texts.

There are about a dozen extant manuscripts of the *Confession*, the earliest of which is contained in the *Book of Armagh*. This was copied by Ferdomnach, the Scribe of Armagh, who died *c*.845. The other manuscripts were preserved in English and continental libraries and date from the tenth to the twelfth centuries. Problems arise because Patricius wrote the *Confession* and the *Letter to Coroticus* for reasons of his own, and those are not the same reasons why we read them today. We want to know when and where he was born and brought up, where he was ordained, what Britain was like when he left it, what Ireland was like when he arrived there, and so on.

Both the *Confession* and the *Letter* were written when Patricius was well established in his Irish mission. The *Confession* is a reply to certain detractors who had been suggesting that Patricius was neither learned nor competent enough to hold the office of Bishop of Hibernia. It is of a later date than the *Letter to Coroticus*, but probably not much later.

Patricius sent a letter to Coroticus because, although nominally a Christian, Coroticus had raided the Irish coast and slaughtered or taken captive a batch of newly baptized Christians, with 'the chrism still gleaming on their foreheads'. Any information that Patricius gives about himself in the course of the ensuing tongue-lashing is entirely incidental.

In the *Confession*, Patricius is writing for people who know a great deal about him already, and only mentions his life history to stress that he was a freeman of noble birth, and to explain his lack of formal education.

More problems were caused for scholars until quite recent times by the rustic Latin that Patricius uses. It is now accepted that Patricius was not writing bad classical Latin: he was writing Latin as it was spoken at the time. His style is that of the spoken language, not that of literature – the exact opposite of the practice of his continental contemporaries. Moreover, it is not his daily spoken language: Patricius used far more Irish in his Irish mission than Latin. His Latin, besides being rustic, is also decidedly rusty.

He was, apparently, a man who did not write any more than he absolutely had to, although it is easy to gather from these two texts that he must have been a powerful preacher. He is well aware that his Latin is below the standards of the people he is addressing – 'you men of letters on your estates'. But, time and again, he stresses that he is not being presumptuous by taking it on himself to convert the Irish. He is indeed the most unworthy of all men, but he cannot help what he is doing because God has chosen him for the mission.

Before extracting what there is in the way of biography from the *Confession* and the *Letter*, it is worth taking a few minutes to read an extract from the *Confession* in Ludwig Bieler's translation, which succeeds in conveying the rather stumbling and clumsy way in which Patricius expresses his thoughts:

For this reason I long had in mind to write, but hesitated until now; I was afraid of exposing myself to the talk of men, because I have not studied like the others, who thoroughly imbibed law and Sacred Scripture, and never had to change from the language of their childhood days, but were able to make it still more perfect . . .

As a youth, nay, almost as a boy not able to speak, I was taken captive, before I knew what to pursue and what to avoid. Hence today I blush and fear exceedingly to reveal my lack of education; for I am unable to tell my story to those versed in the art of concise writing – in such a way, I mean, as my spirit and mind long to do, and so that the sense of my words expresses what I feel . . .

Whence I, once rustic, exiled, unlearned, who does not know how to provide for the future, this at least I know most certainly that before I was humiliated I was like a stone lying in the deep mire; and He that is mighty came and in His mercy lifted me up, and raised me aloft, and placed me on the top of the wall. And therefore I ought to cry out aloud and so also render something to the Lord for his great benefits here and in eternity – benefits which the mind of men is unable to appraise.

Wherefore, then, be astonished, ye great and little that fear God, and you men of letters on your estates, listen and pore over this. Who was it who roused up me, the fool that I am, from the midst of those who in the eyes of men are wise, and expert in law, powerful in word and in everything? And He inspired me – me, the outcast of this world – before others, to be the man (if only I could!) who, with fear and reverence and without blame, should faithfully serve the people to whom the love of Christ conveyed and gave me for the duration of my life, if I should be worthy; yes indeed, to serve them humbly and sincerely . . .

Patricius starts his *Confession* in a spirit of humiliation – he is a sinner, very unlearned, the least of all the faithful and despised by many. We know from contemporary continental writings that such terms were in most cases pious conventions, but with Patricius they are more than that: he does seem to believe quite sincerely that he is 'rusticissimus' and goes to some lengths to explain why one so rustic and unlearned is competent to be Bishop of Hibernia.

Patricius tells us that his father, Calpornius, was a deacon, the son of Potitus, a priest. There was nothing unusual at the time in his immediate ancestors being in holy orders: celibacy was not enforced in the early church. But in the *Letter to Coroticus* he says that his father was a decurion. This is not, however, as inconsistent as might seem. Decurions were men of property who were allocated the civic duty of collecting taxes in their district, never a pleasant task in any time or place. What made it worse for decurions was that they were personally responsible for the taxes, and what could not be collected had to be made good out of their own wealth. An excellent way of ridding oneself of a decurion's burdensome chores was to enter holy orders and become a deacon. Hence, perhaps, the reason for Calpornius's transformation from decurion to deacon.

Patricius then tells us that his father owned a farm or villa (*villula*) near the village of 'Bannavem Taberniae'. This is the only clue to the much-disputed matter of the saint's birthplace. As luck would have it, some scribe along the way, or several of them, miscopied the name. Some scholars reckon it should be 'Bannaventa Taburniae', but this is still no help in locating it. Others take the very sensible attitude that, as the village was already unknown by the year 700, when the first biographies of Patricius were being written, there is not much point in quibbling over how to spell it, and no point whatever in trying to identify it precisely until some fresh evidence comes along.

There is no such village on any map of Roman Britain, nor is there any name close to it. There is no other reference to it apart from the one in the *Confession*. However this has not deterred succeeding generations of Patrician scholars from doing their utmost to identify the birthplace of Patricius. Thirst for knowledge is undoubtedly a good thing, but so is the ability to admit ignorance. The majority of those who take off on a Bannavem Taberniae hunt quickly lose sight of the fact that Patricius never actually says that he was born there, merely that his father had a villa near the place, and that it was while staying at the villa that he was taken captive and sold in slavery to the Irish.

Because Patricius was captured by Irish raiders it seems logical to place Bannavem Taberniae somewhere on the west coast of Britain. The Irish would have been unlikely to raid the east coast, and it is also unlikely that they penetrated far inland. Until very recently there was no archaeological evidence for the existence of villas on or near the north-west coast of Britain at this time, and a location somewhere near the Severn estuary was considered a broadly acceptable solution to the riddle. However, in the past few years, evidence for Roman villas near Strathclyde has emerged, and academic opinion is now favouring the Strathclyde area.

This is how Patricius describes the raid:

I was then about sixteen years of age. I did not know the true God. I was taken into captivity to Ireland with many thousands of people – and deservedly so, because we turned away from God, and did not keep His commandments, and did not obey our priests, who used to remind us of our salvation. And the Lord brought over us the wrath of His anger and scattered us among many nations, even unto the utmost part of the earth, where now my littleness is placed among strangers.

It is important to understand what the move from Romanized Christian Britain to pagan Ireland must have meant for a young man like Patricius. Whatever the state of the continental Empire at that time, Britain was still enjoying the benefits of Roman civilization. Britain had cities, roads to link them, and Roman-style buildings with the usual amenities: stone walls, paved floors, plumbing, baths and even, in some cases, central heating. We do not know exactly how luxurious Patricius's home was. His father, being a decurion, was a reasonably wealthy man. Patricius admits to behaviour that one associates in any age with privileged children who do not need to pull themselves up the social or economic ladder by their own efforts – behaviour such as paying little attention to teachers and not obeying the priests. If Patricius's education (or rather lack of it) was typical of what one scholar calls 'the *jeunesse dorée* of his town', then it is reasonable to assume that his home was fairly comfortable and possessed at least some of the available modern conveniences.

Imagine, then, Patricius's dismay at being abducted to primitive, pagan Ireland and sent to mind sheep (or to herd swine, as some prefer to believe) on a hillside for an unimportant local chieftain. For a Romano-Briton like Patricius, to find himself in Ireland of the early fifth century would have been equivalent to travelling back in time some 400 years. Patricius must have found the chieftain's own lifestyle primitive and uncomfortable: no wonder he turned to prayer and penance when he discovered the conditions he himself, as a slave, would have to put up with.

It is in some quarters the fashion in descriptions of early Irish society to emphasize those features of which modern Ireland can be proud – the well-ordered hierarchical structure, the elaborate kinship system, the complexity of the Brehon laws, the rigours of the poetry school, the stirring beauty of the myths and legends, the highly skilled ornamental metalwork, the courage of the warriors and so on.

But we are not interested in the glories of early Irish society here: we are interested in what Patricius saw when he returned to Ireland as a missionary. He saw a country inhabited by pagan barbarians, and was not impressed. He says virtually nothing about native society in his writings, except to make clear that, much as he loves his Irish Christians, he considers his 'exile' in Ireland as the ultimate sacrifice demanded of him by God, the price he has to pay for his glorious mission. He sums up the achievement of his mission as follows, with one of the few references to the society he found in Ireland:

> Hence, how did it come to pass in Ireland that those who never had a knowledge of God, but until now always worshipped idols and things impure, have now been made a people of the Lord, and are called sons of God, that the sons and daughters of the kings of the Irish are seen to be monks and virgins of Christ?

Patricius learned enough about the Irish social system to exploit its structure for his own proselytizing ends (i.e., convert the chief and the rest will follow), but nowhere does he consider the customs of these pagans worthy of detailed description.

It has been said that Irish history dates from the arrival of Patricius. 'Since the historian depends mainly on written documents for his knowledge of the past,' writes Tomás, Cardinal Ó Fiaich, 'Irish history properly speaking must begin with St Patrick, the author of the earliest documents known to have been written in Ireland.' The use of writing (apart, of course, from ogham inscriptions) only became established in Ireland after the Christian mission had taken a strong hold, so there is no documentary evidence for the state of the country at the time of Patricius's arrival. Archaeologists have proved that Ireland had been inhabited for at least the previous 3000 years by an agricultural people. Metalworkers had been around for about 2000 years, and the Iron Age was about 1000 years old.

Ireland had been in a state of isolation ever since the (undated) arrival of the Celtic speakers. Not only had Rome left the place unmolested, it had not suffered any invasions by Picts or Germanic tribes either. Ireland was, in effect, totally out of time with continental Europe. What Patricius found was an anachronistic Iron Age society modelled on the Celtic speakers' social order, speaking a language of which modern Irish is a direct descendant, that is to say, a Celtic language.

The basis of society was the extended family – the tribal unit known as the *tuath*. There were no towns. The *tuath*, or small kingdom, was made up of units of extended family plus retainers. They lived in isolated farmsteads defended by a ditch and bank system encircling the dwelling houses. The remains of these ring-forts (*raths*) can be seen today all over Ireland. The buildings within the *raths* were mostly simple, thatched structures with little to offer in the way of comfort. Outside the ring-fort the lower social orders had even simpler dwellings of wattle and turf.

Each *tuath* consisted of a hierarchical aristocratic community which lived under the protection of its ruler – the *rí* (king) or *taoiseach* (chief). There were strata of noblemen below the king. The literati – Brehons, druids and bards – and the craftsmen (*aes dána* – the gifted people), constituted a separate social class and depended on the nobles for patronage. Below the *aes dána* came land-owning commoners, and the social scale descended through labourers, serfs and slaves, the lowest of the low being the female slave, whose value was considered equivalent to three heifers.

The main occupation of the tribe was cattle-breeding. There was no coinage: cattle were the main currency and measure of wealth. Because of its bards, its craft traditions and its legal system, early Irish society had a strong cultural unity, but there was no form at all of political unity and certainly no central administration. Some of the *tuatha* gathered together under a High King, but the office of High King of Ireland was a fairly late development – perhaps fourth century – and seems to have been largely ceremonial.

The Christian monks who, in the centuries after Patricius, wrote down the heroic sagas of oral tradition from which much of our knowledge of early Irish society is gleaned, seem to have drawn the line at describing pagan religious practices. This could well be because the pagan Irish did not have much organized religion at all. There are suggestions of sun-worship, and a great reverence for the dead. There were many sacred rivers, streams and wells, some of which archaeologists have identified by the discovery of votive offerings. They held certain gods in awe – Lug and Dagda for example – but we know virtually nothing about how they worshipped them, if at all.

Whether justly or through ignorance of its subtler aspects, the main impression we have of the religion of pagan Ireland is one of animism dominated by superstition – belief in omens and soothsaying, in the power of the curse, in the efficacy of magic formulae and the power of sacred places.

To suggest that the lack of a strongly organized religion among the Irish, and their susceptibility to superstition, made it relatively easy to convert them to Christianity does not necessarily disparage the achievement of Patricius and his helpers and successors. It seems quite likely that the Irish were more innately disposed to accept the doctrines and practices of Christianity than were other cultures. Whatever the reason, it cannot be denied that the people of Ireland gave Christianity an unusually enthusiastic reception. There is not a single martyrdom recorded in the whole history of the conversion of the island, although Patricius tells us that he lived in daily expectation of 'murder, fraud or captivity'. Neither is there any record of violence erupting between the Christians and those who preferred to stay pagan.

Kenneth Neil, the historian, has drawn some interesting conclusions about the relationship between the native religion and the mission of Patricius:

No matter how great the force of Patrick's personality, other factors must have played a part in the amazingly rapid conversion of the Irish. The fact that the indigenous religion was pantheistic and not tied to strict doctrine helped immeasurably; from the beginning the Celts seem to have been willing to accept Christ as just another divinity, thereby giving early missionaries a valuable foothold. Natural events also worked in their favour. A great plague struck Ireland during the 540s, killing up to half the population and probably convincing many of the survivors that the new religion offered their only hope for the future.

It is remarkable that those missionaries who followed Patricius showed none of the hostility to native lore and tradition which is customary in the proselytizing Christian. Patricius himself seems less tolerant of pagan practices than do some of his successors. By the ninth century monks were composing poems in the vernacular and commissioning church ornaments in the 'pagan' (*La Tène*) style.

Patricius could have added immeasurably to our knowledge of pre-Christian Ireland, had that been his intention. It is one of history's great ironies that a document preserved with such care down the centuries takes exactly the knowledge that we are seeking for granted, and proceeds instead to expound on the spiritual experiences of its author:

> But after I came to Ireland – every day I had to tend sheep, and many times a day I prayed – the love of God and His fear came to me more and more, and my faith was strengthened. And my spirit was moved so that in a single day I would say as many as a hundred prayers, and almost as many in the night, and this even when I was staying in the woods and on the mountain; and I used to get up for prayer before daylight, through snow, through frost, through rain, and I felt no harm, and there was no sloth in me – as I now see, because the spirit within me was then fervent.
>
> And there one night I heard in my sleep a voice saying to me: 'It is well that you fast, soon you will go to your own country.' And again, after a short while, I heard a voice saying to me: 'See, your ship is ready.' And it was not near, but at a distance of perhaps two hundred miles, and I had never been there, nor did I know a living soul there; and then I took to flight, and I left the man with whom I had stayed for six years. And I went in the strength of God who directed my way to my good, and I feared nothing until I came to that ship.

*

Six years tending sheep on a mountain was enough to turn the carefree Romano-British youth into a deeply religious 22-year-old, who already has the steadfast faith in his God which characterizes the elder Patricius. On a word from God he finds the courage to travel 200 miles from the place of his captivity to the place where he found the promised ship.

Patricius tells us that when he arrived at the ship he told the captain that he could pay for his journey, but the captain refused to take him on board. But as Patricius was walking away from the ship, praying desperately, one of the men shouted to him to come back, and he was taken aboard.

The man said to Patricius: 'Come, hurry, we shall take you on in good faith; make friends with us in whatever way you like.' And Patricius continues: 'And so on that day I refused to suck their breasts for fear of God, but rather hoped they would come to the faith of Jesus Christ because they were pagans.' Does the phrase 'on that day' imply that Patricius had previously indulged in the native rite of the sucking of breasts to symbolize the giving and receiving of protection, but desisted on this occasion because his journey had been dictated by the Lord? Whether it does or not, the casual comment certainly shows how alien Irish society of the time was to anything Patricius would have known in Roman Britain.

Patricius takes up the story again:

. . . we set sail at once. And after three days we reached land, and for twenty-eight days we travelled through deserted country. And they lacked food, and hunger overcame them; and the next day the captain said to me: 'Tell me, Christian: you say that your God is great and all-powerful; why, then, do you not pray for us? As you can see, we are suffering from hunger; it is unlikely indeed that we shall ever see a human being again.'

I said to them full of confidence: 'Be truly converted with all your heart to the Lord my God, because nothing is impossible for Him, that this day He may send you food on your way until you be satisfied; for He has abundance everywhere.' And, with the help of God, so it came to pass: suddenly a herd of pigs appeared on the road before our eyes, and they killed many of them; and there they stopped for two nights and fully recovered their strength, and their hounds received their fill, for many of them had grown weak and were half-dead along the way. And from that day they had plenty of food. They also found wild honey, and offered some of it to me.

It has often been pointed out that it is typical of Patricius's way of telling a story that he does not mention the hounds at the beginning of the ship episode, but only incidentally, and in the middle of the story. Irish wolfhounds, massive creatures, were greatly prized on the Continent in the fifth century, and this colourful detail of the *Confession* – that the ship bearing Patricius out of imprisonment was carrying a cargo of wolfhounds – is historically plausible. Symmachus, writing shortly before this time, says that Irish hounds were brought as far as Rome to be exhibited in public games. The hounds were a generally accepted part of the story until as recently as 1968, when the Anglo-Irish scholar and bishop R. P. C. Hanson pointed out that *canes* in the above passage, which is the one and only mention of dogs in the *Confession*, could be a corruption of *carnes*, 'flesh', a reading which appears in some of the manuscripts. This reading suggests that the flesh (*carnes*) of the pigs filled the men's bellies, and there were never any hounds at all.

Early translations of the *Confession* refer to the country where Patricius landed as a 'desert' – '*per disertum iter fecimus*' ('we made a journey through a desert'). But there were no deserts within three days' sailing of Ireland big enough to travel around in: only sandy patches of coastline. A more likely translation is 'uninhabited (deserted) lands'. It is just about feasible, given the right winds and tides, that a large *currach* of the sort in which Patricius would be travelling could reach the coast of Gaul in three days, but the coast of Britain is a far more likely landing place. Patricius, of course, does not tell us where he landed.

Instead he next tells us of a dream he had on the night of the day that they found food. That he chose to include it in this relatively short *Confession*, written so many years after the event, indicates that it had a great significance for him. Satan, he tells us, tempted him strongly while he was asleep and he felt as if a huge rock had fallen on him and deprived his limbs of all power. He knows not why, but he cried out 'Helias!', and while he cried out the sun arose and its rays removed all the weight from him: 'And I believe that I was sustained by Christ my Lord, and that His spirit was even then crying out in my behalf, and I hope it will be so on the day of my tribulation.'

Patricius himself was puzzled by the word that he chose to call out: 'But whence came it into my mind, ignorant as I am, to call upon Helias?' Helias is Latin for Elijah (vocative Helia), and the classical Greek for the sun is Helios. But it is still difficult to see why this dream should have made such a strong impression on Patricius, and many ingenious interpretations have been offered, most of which only serve to complicate the issue. The best explanation seems to be the suggestion that the dream-work in Patricius's half-conscious imagination was confusing the prophet Elijah, who had a very high status in early Christian times, with the sun god Helios.

The tedious and tortuous debate about Helias is nothing compared to the amount of intellectual ingenuity that has been expended on the next two verses of the *Confession*:

> And once again after many years, I fell into captivity. On that first night I stayed with them. I heard a divine message saying to me: 'Two months will you be with them.' And so it came to pass: on the sixtieth night thereafter the Lord delivered me out of their hands.
>
> Also on our way God gave us food and fire and dry weather every day, until, on the tenth day, we met people. As I said above, we travelled twenty-eight days through deserted country, and the night that we met people we had no food left.

The debate that has arisen about the number of days that Patricius and the ship's crew spent wandering in the 'desert' is partly due to the imprecision of his Latin. One school of thought maintains that Patricius and the crew travelled together for 28 days, in the midst of which they were held captive by hostile natives for a period of 60 days, and afterwards were either released or made their escape. The other school of thought insists that the 60 days' captivity which Patricius recalls here happened to him much later in life, during his Irish mission, and is mentioned at this point because the sensation of relief experienced in his 'Helias' dream reminded him of the relief he felt at his deliverance then.

Similar difficulties have been caused by Patricius's next statement:

> And again after a few years I was in Britain with my people, who received me as their son, and sincerely besought me that now at last, having suffered so many hardships, I should not leave them and go elsewhere.

It is not clear whether the 'few years' refer to his first six years of captivity or to further adventures with the seafarers. Nor is it certain whether the *parentes* he mentions are his mother and father or simply relatives, although as he implies that his father escaped capture there is no reason why his parents should not still be alive six or ten years later.

It is easy to imagine how glad Patricius must have been to arrive back home. But he was not to stay there long: God was about to call him to a new and lasting 'captivity' among the heathens from whom he had just escaped:

> And there I saw in the night the vision of a man, whose name was Victoricus, coming as it were from Ireland, with countless letters. And he gave me one of them, and I read the opening words of the letter, which were, 'The voice of the Irish'; and as I read the beginning of the letter I thought that at the same moment I heard their voice – they were those beside the Wood of Voclut, which is near the Western Sea – and thus did they cry out as with one mouth: 'We ask thee, boy, come and walk among us once more.'
>
> And I was quite broken in heart, and could read no further, and so I woke up. Thanks be to God, after many years the Lord gave them according to their cry.

There is no way of knowing who Victoricus was, but, inevitably, there is no lack of ingenious suggestions. The same applies to the location of the Wood of Voclut. Nor does Patricius follow this paragraph by a description of his preparation for his mission to the Irish. Instead this dream marks the point where the short, more or less chronological section of the *Confession* ends and, as far as its author is concerned, the real business in hand begins.

From this point on Patricius is pleading his case: defending his divine vocation which has apparently been cast in doubt, and his missionary practices which were also criticized. Any further information that can be gleaned from Patricius about his life and times is even more incidental than before.

The dream of Victoricus reminds Patricius of other occasions on which God came to his aid in 'a vision of the night'. There are, in all, eight such visions in his writings, all remarkable for their simplicity and their convincing but unspectacular dream-logic. They contrast strikingly with the stereotyped 'visions' of other early saints, which often seem to have been embroidered with appropriately portentous symbolic elements after the event.

We have already looked at his 'Helias' dream, which obviously impressed him far more than it impresses us. The same is true of the incidents described in Chapters 24 and 25 of the *Confession*. They do, however, give a wonderful sense of Patricius's modesty and humility. Far from boasting that he has felt the presence of the Lord, he continually thanks the Lord for having chosen to reveal himself to one so unworthy – 'a stone raised up from the mire and set on top of the wall' – and marvels at his good fortune.

The Lord also chose to help Patricius in a humiliating ordeal involving some of his ecclesiastical superiors, and this is what he tells us about next. A sin committed at about the age of 15 which he confessed to his spiritual adviser and friend while a deacon, was held against him 30 years later (30 years after having confessed it or after having committed it? – Patricius's Latin is not clear on this point, though the latter seems more likely). The friend had promised to recommend Patricius for episcopal rank, but instead he revealed Patricius's youthful sin to the assembled ecclesiastics. It was only the strength of God's comfort that carried Patricius through the humiliation. After the ordeal he had another 'vision of the night', in which God comforted him in such a way as to give the impression that He was on Patricius's side. He sums up the experience by saying that it felt as if God had told him (in the words of the Scriptures), 'He who toucheth you toucheth as it were the apple of my eye.' It is not difficult to imagine how overawed the humble Patricius must have been by such a dream.

Patricius goes on to say that besides thanking God for the strength given to him, he also forgives the friend who betrayed him. We do not know who his friend was, and neither do we know what the sin was, but that has not deterred successive generations of scholars from having a good guess.

The 22-year-old recently escaped slave (about 45 years old, if one accepts that the sin's commission and not its confession was referred to by the phrase '30 years later') has now become not only a deacon, but a member of the clergy and under consideration for a bishopric. It is important to remember that he gives no information in his authentic historical writings about his further education, his preparation for ordination or his life as a priest.

Most scholars would have him educated in Gaul, but more up-to-date opinion, informed by the great growth of our knowledge of fifth-century Britain and Ireland that has taken place in the last twenty years, has built an excellent case for a British education and ordination. There are, however, hints in both the *Confession* and *Coroticus* that Patricius had visited Gaul. In the *Letter to Coroticus* he refers to the Gaulish practice of redeeming captives. The monastic life began to flourish in Gaul under St Martin of Tours in 360 and was attracting large numbers of recruits; their fervently devout ascetic life would hold great appeal for a man like Patricius. Towards the end of the *Confession* he expresses a longing to 'visit the brethren' in Gaul, but his dedication to his mission prevents him from doing so:

Wherefore, then, even if I wished to leave them and go to Britain – and how I would have loved to go to my country and my parents, and also to Gaul in order to visit the brethren and to see the face of the saints of my Lord! God knows it that I much desired it; but I am bound by the Spirit, who gives evidence against me if I do this, telling me that I shall be guilty; and I am afraid of losing the labour which I have begun – nay, not I, but Christ the Lord who bade me come here and stay with them for the rest of my life.

Patricius never loses his identity as a Roman Briton, much as he loves and cares about his Irish Christians. Ireland is seen throughout the *Confession* and *Coroticus* as a place of exile. His presence there remains a form of 'captivity': 'I dwell in the midst of barbarians, a stranger and exile for the love of God.'

But his exile has its reward: the conversion of the Irish. He has, he tells us, baptized 'many thousands of men'. As a result of his labours a Christian Church was growing up in a pagan country: 'I have not laboured for nothing, and my journeying abroad has not been in vain . . . the sons and daughters of the kings of the Irish are seen to be monks and virgins of Christ.'

Patricius tells us about a 'blessed Irishwoman of noble birth' who decided to become a nun; he expresses concern for the state of Christian Irish slaves, and admiration for their courage in embracing the new religion. He also mentions that Irish men and women are helping him in his mission: 'clerics are ordained for them [the Irish] everywhere.' But apart from Coroticus, and the messenger Victoricus, no one else is mentioned by name in his writings.

Much of the later part of the *Confession* is taken up with oblique protestations of innocence on Patricius's part in reply to accusations or rumours that he had been either wasting money sent from Britain or hoarding money donated to him in Ireland. Whatever the charge was, it is clear enough that Patricius was deeply offended by it, and his protestations of innocence certainly ring true.

The ending of the *Confession* is one of the most carefully composed parts, but still Patricius cannot resist making two more references to his lack of education:

I pray those who believe and fear God, whosoever deigns to look at or receive this writing which Patricius, a sinner, unlearned, has composed in Ireland, that no one should ever say that it was my ignorance if I did or showed forth anything however small according to God's good pleasure; but let this be your conclusion and let it so be thought, that – as is the perfect truth – it was the gift of God. This is my confession before I die.

The *Letter to Coroticus* is about one-third of the length of the *Confession*. Coroticus was a nominally Christian chieftain, living either in Wales or, as modern academics tend to believe, in the Strathclyde area. The *Letter* begins with sentiments familiar to us from the *Confession*:

I, Patricius, a sinner, unlearned, resident in Ireland, declare myself to be a bishop. Most assuredly I believe that what I am I have received from God. And so I live among barbarians, a stranger and exile for the love of God. He is witness that this is so. Not that I wished my mouth to utter anything so hard and harsh; but I am forced by the zeal for God; and the truth of Christ has wrung it from me, out of love for my neighbours and sons for whom I gave up my country and parents and my life to the point of death. If I be worthy, I live for my God to teach the heathen, even though some may despise me.

The letter is 'hard and harsh' because its purpose is to excommunicate Coroticus. Patricius has already sent a letter by messenger to Coroticus asking him to return the newly baptized Christians whom he had abducted – in a manner more fitting to 'fellow citizens of the demons' than to 'citizens of the holy Romans' – and Coroticus and his soldiers had laughed at the request.

Patricius writes both in anger and in grief: first because his beloved newly baptized Christians have been cruelly abducted (and among them women, who are likely to be sexually abused by the men of Coroticus), and also because the crime was carried out by a chieftain who was himself nominally a Christian. He demands not only the return of his Christians, but also that Coroticus and his men undertake serious penance in reparation for their crime. He uses his authority as Bishop of Ireland to excommunicate Coroticus and his followers, and berates him so fiercely that at several points his Latin becomes incomprehensible:

Where, then will Coroticus with his criminals, rebels against Christ, where will they see themselves, they who distribute baptized women as prizes – for a miserable temporal kingdom, which will pass away in a moment? As a cloud of smoke that is dispersed by the wind, so shall the deceitful wicked perish at the presence of the Lord . . .

As in the *Confession*, Patricius frequently resorts to biblical quotations in order to express himself. He does this so often in the *Letter* that one learned commentator has described Patricius's method of chastisement as 'flinging the Latin Bible at the head of his opponents'.

The *Letter* is without any doubt from the same pen as the *Confession*. Above all it illustrates what a powerful preacher Patricius must have been when aroused. It adds little in the way of biography to our picture of Patricius, but it does bring the man vividly to life, and also shows the sort of outrages he had to deal with in his ministry.

The picture of the historical Patricius is, therefore, strong on characterization, but decidedly lacking in matters of geographical and biographical fact. Chronology has been ignored here because Patricius does not mention any dates himself, but it has been firmly established that these two texts were written in the late fifth century. It is clear that Patricius was born somewhere in Roman Britain, that he spent some years in slavery in Ireland, that he received an ecclesiastical education of some sort, but never recovered from the disruption of his youthful schooling. He called himself Bishop of Ireland, and was recognized as such in Britain, even though he had some detractors there; he baptized many Irish people and provided clergy for them.

Above all, the writings tell us about Patricius the man. He was a man of simple and steadfast faith, humble, hard-working and courageous, with an especially deep and reverential love for his God, a man who never ceased to marvel at having been chosen for such a demanding and rewarding task as the conversion of the Irish.

Nothing more is heard of Patricius for nearly two centuries after his death. The figure who reappears in early medieval Ireland is a far more familiar one than Patricius, recognizably Saint Patrick, the apostle of Ireland, miracle-worker *extraordinaire*. Were it not for the fact that several people in several different places thought it worth while to preserve the writings of the historical Patricius, nothing would have been known of the 'other', historical Saint Patrick, the humble, hard-working, courageous Romano-British bishop, who was so endearingly ashamed of his bad Latin.

2

THE EARLIEST *LIVES* AND
THE LECALE PENINSULA

Patricius in his own writings gives the impression that he laboured alone for the conversion of Ireland, helped only by native clergy ordained by himself, and posterity has taken up this image with a vengeance. This is unfortunate. We can be certain, knowing the humility and sanctity of the character we have chosen to call Patricius, that he did not intend to give the impression that he had converted Ireland single-handed. He was writing in defence of his own Irish mission, and so he only mentions his own activities. A description of the state of the Christian church in Ireland at the time lay just as much outside Patricius's project as did a description of the political state of the country in those days, or of the practices of the pagans.

Christianity had been infiltrating into Ireland through contacts with Britain and Gaul for some time. Most scholars accept AD 432 as the date of Patricius's arrival in Ireland as a missionary, and 461 as the date of his death. The alternative dates are either 432 or 461 for his arrival and 492 for his death, giving him, like Moses, a lifespan of 120 years in the case of the 432–92 dates.

The little that we know of the missionaries who were working in Ireland before Saint Patrick's time suggests that they were all active in the midlands and the south of the country, while Patrick was based in Ulster. Patricius specifically states in his *Confession* that he travelled to parts 'where Christians were not', usually taken to mean that there were no Christians in the whole of Ireland. It now looks more likely that he is referring to Ulster and Connaught – the north and north-west parts of the country – and that there were probably Gaulish Christian missions well established in the midlands and on the south-east coast.

Tradition has associated Patrick with Secundinus, alias

Sechnaill, who was working in Meath, and with Auxilius who left a foundation near Naas in Co. Kildare. Traditionally they are believed to be fellow bishops of Patrick, ordained by him to help in his mission. A beautiful hymn in praise of Saint Patrick is attributed (erroneously it is now believed) to Secundinus, who predeceased Patrick. Leaving tradition to one side, it seems more likely that, rather than being subordinate bishops converted and ordained by Patrick (and in spite of the subordinate positions suggested, coincidentally, by their names), Auxilius and Secundinus had established Christian communities in Ireland before the arrival of Patrick. The latest (1987) theory suggests that Auxilius and Secundinus were part of a fairly large mission which had earlier come over from Gaul to convert the Irish.[1] This theory might also explain the cults which appear to have existed before St Patrick's time to Saints Ciaran, Declan and Ailbe in Munster.

There are many legends concerning these saints, some of which are duplicates of legends also associated with Patrick and other, later, saints. It is most likely that Ciaran, Declan and Ailbe are composite figures, overlapping at times with the more famous Patrick. It does not look as if we shall ever have any historical facts about the early Irish saints: all that we can know for certain from later legend is that their sanctity impressed people sufficiently for their names to live on in folk memory and to become firmly associated with certain places.

As well as the Gaulish mission, there is evidence of contacts between the Irish and Christians in Wales and Britain. There were Irish settlements in Christian Wales in the early fifth century. Given the short sea crossing there was probably a fair amount of traffic between Wales and the south-east coast of Ireland at the time. We know that the pagan Irish were in the habit of raiding the coast of Britain when in need of slaves, and carrying off significant numbers of Christians many of whom, like Patricius, must have found great solace in their religion in their new circumstances. Etymological evidence indicates, as early as the fifth century, a British origin for many religious words in Old Irish such as Easter, priest, veil and vespers. Archaeological evidence suggests that there was trading between ports on the south-east and south-west coasts of Ireland and the west coast of Britain and Wales.

It is now generally accepted that Patrick was not responsible for the single-handed conversion of Ireland. So is the existence of a series of important factors which predisposed Irish society towards Christianity and led to a conversion unparalleled in Christian history for its lack of bloodshed. This is all the more remarkable when we remember that Ireland was the first country outside the Roman Empire to be converted. The early missionaries followed a policy later endorsed by Pope Gregory I (590–604) which encouraged missionaries to graft Christianity on to whatever forms of prevailing religion existed: for example, the Celtic harvest festival, *Samhain*, was replaced by All Saints' Day. Many of the customs associated with the celebration of Hallowe'en on 31 October are believed to be a legacy of this fusion of Celtic and Christian festivals.

We have only one external corroboration of the existence of Christianity in Ireland before the arrival of Patrick. Prosper of Aquitaine says in his Chronicle that in 431: 'To the Irish believing in Christ, Palladius is commissioned by Pope Celestine as their first bishop.' According to the usually reliable Prosper, there were enough Christians in Ireland by 431 (one year before the earliest suggested date of Patrick's mission) for the Pope to consider it worth while sending them a bishop. Bishops were not, at that time, sent to convert – a priest was good enough for that: bishops were sent to impose episcopal order on an already sizeable Christian community.

Palladius is also mentioned in the Irish Annals – those of Ulster and Innisfallen. But, significantly, the Annals fail to mention that Palladius was sent to 'the Irish believing in Christ':

AD 431: Palladius is commissioned to the Irish by Celestine, bishop of Rome, and sent to Ireland as their first bishop in order that they may believe in Christ. (*Annals of Innisfallen*)

The Irish Annals, it must be remembered, were compiled at a much later date. By the time they were written down, the legend of Patrick's single-handed conversion of Ireland was already well established, and it would not have been a popular move to mention the existence of a large Christian community on the island before the arrival of the mighty Patrick.

Whatever the reason for the discrepancy in one detail between Prosper of Aquitaine and the Irish Annals, all the annalists agree that in 432 a bishop called Patricius was appointed to the Irish. We do not know what happened to Palladius, whether he died a natural death shortly after his arrival, or was killed by the heathen Irish, or simply abandoned an uncongenial task and resumed his episcopal career in some more promising setting. According to tradition, he died in Britain on his way to visit the Picts.

The establishment of Saint Patrick as the figure who was single-handedly responsible for the conversion of Ireland begins with the work of Muirchú and Tirechán, seventh-century hagiographers based in Armagh. Hagiography – the writing of the lives of the saints – is a specialized literary genre. The fantastic miracles and feats of endurance attributed in such writings to both early Christian and medieval saints are not much to the liking of modern readers, not even the most devout. There is a strong impulse to dismiss these repetitive accounts of far-fetched miracles and outlandish exploits as the product of gullible and over-zealous scribes. The Vatican, no less, has endorsed this tendency by its recent 'demotion' of such well-loved figures as the efficacious patron of travellers ex-Saint Christopher, and also of George, the patron saint of England. Saint Patrick is among that select band who were recognized as saints before the practice of canonization was introduced. When Ulrich, the first person to be officially canonized by papal authority, was declared a saint in 993, Patrick had already been a saint for over 500 years – canonized by the *vox populi*, the consensus of the Irish people.

Hagiography is neither history nor biography, but neither is it entirely legend and fancy. It is a form of glorifying and perpetuating the memory of a saint by the means of awe-inspiring and edifying tales based on his or her life. Besides being a devotional aid, saints' lives were also a means of legitimizing their prestige and establishing their importance as representatives of Christ. At times baser political motives were involved – when one faction of the church needed to enhance the prestige of its patron saint in order to assert its supremacy over a rival faction.

Miraculous and marvellous stories are repeated over and over again in early Christian hagiography and attributed to different saints with only minor variations. Miracles can be classified in much the same way that the limited stock of motifs have been classified in folk-tales. Indeed, such folk-tales often appear in hagiography disguised as miracles.

The most interesting miracles in Irish hagiography are those in which the saint's actions demonstrate the superiority of Christian religion over pagan superstition. The saint at times takes on the characteristics of a hero of Irish saga, even though such characteristics are not consonant with Christian practice, in order to enhance his or her status, and also, one suspects, to keep the audience amused. The saint is a new kind of hero, and people would expect him or her to behave like one.

The saint also inherits the magical powers of the druid, whose status he is assuming. He exhibits mastery over nature. Fire, water, air, the weather, fishes and wild animals all respond to the saint's commands. The saint develops a special relationship with birds and animals, assuming the form of a beast on occasion.

The two earliest *Lives* of Patrick – those of Muirchú (pronounced *Murra-hoo*) and Tirechán (pronounced *Teera-hawn*) – were written *c.* 665–80, that is, about 200 years after the death of Patrick. They combine biographical material selectively culled from the *Confession* with material which had, in the course of those 200 years, grown up around the saint in the oral tradition. Compared with the productions of later hagiographers, Muirchú and Tirechán are relatively restrained; nevertheless, many of the later, more extravagant stories can be traced back to them.

Both Muirchú and Tirechán were working for an elder bishop. Muirchú's patron was Bishop Aedh of Sletty, in Co. Carlow, and Tirechán was a pupil of Bishop Ultán of Ardbraccan in Co. Meath. Aedh and Ultán are considered by many scholars to be an important source of early oral tradition for the younger scribes. Both Muirchú and Tirechán acknowledge their patrons as sources of information about Patrick. This new information, not to be found in the *Confession* and appearing for the first time in these seventh-century *Lives*, is referred to as 'traditional'.

Tirechán's account of Patrick was probably written in the 660s, and predates Muirchú's *Life*. However, Tirechán was not so much writing a life of Patrick as compiling a record of Patrick's travels through Meath and Connaught. Because Muirchú's more-or-less chronological narrative is more important for the development of the Patrick legend, his *Life* will be considered first and in greater detail than Tirechán's.

The flurry of hagiographical activity in the late seventh century, of which Muirchú's work forms an important part, was closely linked to certain controversies which had arisen among Irish Christians. Muirchú's work was designed to further the interests of Armagh and the northern Christians in the resolution of these controversies – the first example of Saint Patrick's life being rewritten in the interests of propaganda.

Differences of opinion and practice had arisen between the more British and Gaulish influenced church of the south of Ireland and the relatively isolated Celtic church in the north, over such matters as the correct form of tonsure and how to calculate the date of Easter. The Celtic church insisted on shaving the front hair and letting the hair at the back of the head grow long. They also refused to follow the papal ruling adopted by the rest of western Christianity for calculating the date of Easter. Armagh seems to have ceded to the majority opinion in these matters in return for being recognized as the dominant see – the archbishopric – of the Irish church.

Furthermore, the clerics of Armagh were backing the claims of the Uí Neill monarchs who were basing their bid for supremacy over other provincial monarchs by promoting a legendary High-Kingship of Tara and asserting that the monarch who held Tara (a member of Uí Neill at the time) could claim to be monarch of all Ireland. This is one reason why Tara is so dominant in Muirchú's account of Patrick.

Armagh based its claim to supremacy on the fact that Saint Patrick, who was responsible for the conversion of Ireland, had chosen Armagh as the headquarters of his church. The current incumbents were therefore his direct heirs. As its patron, Patrick, was the dominant saint, so Armagh was the dominant see.

It is quite probable that there were many Christians in Ireland at this date, especially in Munster, who had only vaguely heard of Saint Patrick, if at all. Robin Flower, the pioneering scholar of early Irish literature, finds no evidence for a cult of Saint Patrick before the eighth century: 'if we study the lives of the saints of the sixth and seventh centuries we find that Colmcille is to these writers the typical Irish saint far more than Patrick, who in these records is a somewhat intermittent and shadowy figure.'[2] So besides promoting Patrick as founder and patron of Armagh, it was also necessary to establish him beyond any doubt as the apostle and patron saint of Ireland.

Muirchú's life of Patrick is interesting as much for what it leaves out as for the new elements that it adds to the story. Gone is the humble, self-deprecating Patricius with his strong but simple faith and fatherly concern for his newly converted Christians, the man who 'lived daily in fear of murder, fraud or captivity'. Instead we have a wonder-working druid proceeding around the country with a vast retinue converting and/or outwitting all who cross his path. Patricius disappears and another man emerges from the land of legend. As the historian D. A. Binchy has so rightly said: 'It is hardly necessary to add that the effect of such legends is the exact opposite of what their framers had in mind: far from glorifying Patrick, they diminish his stature. Indeed, had his own writings perished, his biographers would have effectively obscured the real greatness of the man.'[3] And, no doubt, the Vatican would have seen fit to demote him.

Muirchú introduces the traditional (or should it be apocryphal?) material upon whose acceptance or rejection our picture of the topographical and biographical details of Patrick's life so largely depends.

He begins with a précis of Patrick's *Confession* which at times follows the original word for word. Muirchú concentrates on facts that can be gleaned from the *Confession*, leaving out any reference to Patrick's humility and lack of learning, a trait on which, as we have seen, Patricius himself is most insistent. He adds that Patrick was also named Sochet, identifies Bannavem

Taberniae as 'Ventre' and names Patrick's mother as Concessa. He mentions Patrick's slavery and escape and his wanderings in the 'desert' with the ship's crew. At this point, and many others in Muirchú, Patrick is compared to Moses, as befits a figure being built up as a patriarch and national apostle.

Muirchú departs from the *Confession* by sending Patrick, at the age of 30, to study in Gaul with Germanus of Auxerre, in Muirchú's time a byword for all that was admired in the monastic life-style. Patrick spent 30 or 40 years there, until his friend Victoricus, who had appeared to him in visions while he was a slave, came to him in a vision to tell him that 'The sons and daughters of the Wood of Voclut are calling you.'

So Patrick set out for Ireland with a senior companion, Segitus, whom Germanus sent with him because Patrick had not yet been consecrated a bishop. Patrick knew that Palladius had been sent to Ireland by Pope Celestine, but, according to Muirchú, Palladius' mission was doomed because 'nobody can receive anything from the earth unless it be given to him from heaven': i.e., Palladius was not divinely destined to convert Ireland: that was Patrick's task.

Patrick was in Ebmoria (an unidentified place) when he heard that Palladius had abandoned his Irish mission and died in Britain. Patrick and his entourage made a detour to 'an admirable and great bishop named Amathorex' who consecrated Patrick as bishop. His companions, Auxilius and Iserninus, were ordained to lower grades. They boarded ship forthwith for Ireland, 'for nobody seeks the Lord with sloth'.

Next, Muirchú makes a digression in order to set the scene in Ireland in those days. Loegaire, son of Niall, 'a great king, a fierce pagan, an emperor of non-Romans', held sway over almost the entire island from his seat at Tara. 'He had around him sages and druids, fortune-tellers and sorcerers, and the inventors of every evil craft, who according to the custom of paganism and idolatry, were able to know and foresee everything before it happened.' Loegaire's chief druids, Lochru and Lucet Mael, were frequently prophesying the arrival of a foreigner 'with an unheard-of and burdensome teaching' who would put an end to their way of life. 'These are the words of the poem,' says Muirchú, and adds that it is 'not very intelligible, owing to the peculiarity of their language':

> There shall arrive Shaven-head,
> with his stick bent in the head,
> from his house with a hole in its head
> he will chant impiety
> from his table in the front of his house;
> all his people will answer 'Be it thus, be it thus.'

Loegaire's druids in fact gave us the first pictorial representation of Patrick: he is tonsured in the Roman style (shaved bald), carrying the bishop's crozier, wearing a Roman-style cloak with a hole in its centre for the head, and saying Mass on an altar outside his house while his people answer 'Amen'.

Muirchú then returns to Patrick, whose ship has arrived at the port of Inber Dee. Having made his landfall, Patrick decided that as he was still technically a fugitive slave, he should first go north to buy himself free (with a double ransom) from his pagan master, Miliucc. He sailed up the coast and landed at Inber Slane, where he met Dichu who became his first convert. There is now, Muirchú says, a barn (*sabhall* in Irish) named after Patrick in this place. He stayed with Dichu for a few days, then set off by land to Slemish 'from which mountain a long time ago, when he was serving there as a captive, he had seen the angel Victoricus leave the imprint of his swift step on the rock of another mountain, and ascend into heaven before his eyes.' Victoricus, the 'friend' of the *Confession*, turns into an angel at this stage.

Miliucc heard that his former slave was on his way to visit him to force him to change his way of life so 'he gathered all his wealth together in the palace where until then he had lived as king, and burnt himself along with it.' Such was the pagan custom when faced with inevitable defeat. Patrick is so outraged at Miliucc's action – preferring to immolate himself as a pagan instead of choosing to serve eternal God – that he curses him: 'God knows, none of his sons shall sit on his throne as king of his kingdom in generations to come; what is more, his line shall be subordinate for ever.'

Next comes a long description of Patrick's triumph over Loegaire at Tara as he celebrates Ireland's first Easter. This marks Muirchú's entry into the world of 'native' legend. Germanus, Dichu and Miliucc may be just so much non-historical tradition, but at least they are not fantastic like Loegaire and his druids.

Patrick and his entourage decided that they should celebrate Easter near Tara because that was the place where the greatest kingdom among the tribes practised their idolatry. They held their feast on the same night that Patrick intended to celebrate Easter. One of the pagan customs was that on that night nobody should light a fire before a fire appeared in the palace of Tara. Patrick, however, lit the paschal fire in his tent on the plain below. It was observed from the hill of Tara, and the druids told the enraged king that unless the offending fire was extinguished that same night it would never be put out: '. . . it will even rise above all the fires of our customs and he who has kindled it on this night will overpower us all and you, and will seduce all the people of your kingdom, and all kingdoms will yield to it, and it will spread over the whole country and will reign in all eternity.'

So Loegaire ordered 'thrice nine chariots' to be made ready and then set off to investigate. On his druids' advice he waited outside Patrick's tent for the saint to approach him, so that the druids could engage him in dispute. As soon as Patrick appeared one of the druids, Ercc, defected to the Christian camp. Druid Lochru insulted the Christian faith, so Patrick cursed him in the name of the Lord. 'And at these words the druid was lifted up into the air and fell down again; he hit his brain against a stone, and was smashed to pieces, and died in their presence and the pagans stood in fear.'

The king and his companions were furious. When Patrick saw that they were on the verge of attacking him he called on God, who sent an earthquake which wreaked such havoc, flinging chariots, men and horses in all directions, that 'seven times seven men perished'. Only the king and the queen and three others survived. The king, in fear, pretended to do homage, then left, vowing that he would kill Patrick by any means.

Patrick was aware of the 'wicked thoughts of the wicked king', so he blessed his companions – eight men and a boy – and set off after the king. As the king was counting them, they disappeared before his eyes, and all he could see was eight deer with a fawn. The king went back to Tara badly shaken.

The next day, Easter, King Loegaire was celebrating his pagan feast at Tara by feasting, and drinking wine, when Patrick and five companions entered through closed doors – just as Christ did, Muirchú comments. Dubthach, a poet, was the only one who rose to greet him. The pagans then invited Patrick to eat in order, as he knew, to put him to the test.

While they were eating, the druid Lucet Mael put a drop of poison into Patrick's cup. Patrick blessed the cup, the liquor froze solid, and when he turned his goblet upside down only the drops of poison fell out. Then he blessed it again and the liquor unfroze.

The druid was impressed, and invited Patrick to work miracles in contest with him. Patrick asked what sort of miracles, and the druid suggested bringing down snow. Patrick declined, saying that he did not want to bring about anything against God's will. The druid brought down waist-high snow all over the plain. 'All right, we see this. Remove it now,' said Patrick. The druid had to admit he could not do so until the same time tomorrow. 'You can do evil and cannot do good. Not so I,' said Patrick, and he blessed the plain and the snow disappeared. Then the druid brought down fog, and again Patrick had to remove it.

Next the king suggested Patrick and the druid both throw their books in the water, and said he would worship the one whose books remained unharmed. This anachronism – druids did not have books – occurs because the incident has been copied from the legend of the confrontation of Simon Magus and St Peter. The druid refused on the grounds that water was one of Patrick's gods. 'He had heard, no doubt,' says Muirchú, 'that Patrick baptized with water.' The druid declined a contest by fire on the same grounds, so Patrick suggested that the boy Benignus should take part in the trial in his place.

A special house was built for the contest, half of green wood and half of dry wood. Benignus, wearing the druid's garb, went into the dry part. The druid, wearing Patrick's chasuble, was shut up in the green part, then both parts of the building were set on fire. Nothing was left of the druid and the green part of the house except Patrick's chasuble. Benignus and the dry part were unscathed except for the druid's garb which was burned up.

Loegaire was angry at the death of another druid, but God restrained him from attacking Patrick. The saint warned the king that if he did not believe now he would die at once. After a quick word with his surviving druids the king decided to believe, and many others were converted with him. Patrick responded by telling him that 'Since you have resisted my teaching and been offensive to me, the days of your reign shall run on, but none of your offspring shall ever be king.'

The rest of Muirchú's book consists of descriptions of sixteen of Saint Patrick's miracles (see pp. 177–80). They are extremely far-fetched, and vary in interest, but they form the core of Patrick's wonder-working reputation, an important part of his legend.

In Muirchú's life there is a picture of a very different saint from the historical Patricius. Every single trait in his writings which could be interpreted as a sign of weakness, or even plain human-ity, has been excised. The circumstances surrounding the *Letter to Coroticus*, for example, in which the capture and murder of Pat-rick's converts would be seen as a defeat, have been suppressed and replaced by a simple animal-transformation miracle (see no. 2, p. 177).

This early medieval Patrick is, consistently, a man of great stat-ure, if rather uncertain temper. He addresses even the mightiest king in the country as an equal. He is a persistent opponent, and, with the help of God, always gets his own way eventually. His power over the elements easily outstrips that of the druids, even though he refuses to use his powers for the purpose of idle dis-play. He is a master hand at both striking dead and raising from the dead. He is an adept in the art of cursing, and shows a fair amount of vindictiveness. He can change both his opponents and his followers into the form of wild animals. He is, how-ever, kind to his followers and to those who repent and believe. Miracle no. 1, for example, in which the virgin dies immediately after baptism, is meant to imply that her faith is rewarded by instant transference to heaven where she can see the face of God without further earthly trial.

Muirchú also stresses Patrick's great prayerfulness. He recites hymns and psalms and canticles of the Scriptures all day long, and 'signed himself with the victorious sign of the cross a hundred times at every hour of the day and night'. A comparison of Muirchú's statement with Patricius's modest remark in *Confession* that, while he was a slave, in one day he would say 'as many as a hundred prayers, and nearly as many at night . . . because the spirit was fervent within me' shows that the propagandist in Muirchú not only transformed the character of Saint Patrick, but also changed his simple spirituality into a crude and mechanical piety.[4]

It has been suggested that miracles 1–10 were collected by Muirchú from oral sources, while 11–16, which cover Patrick's death and burial, plus the elaborate story of Loegaire's conversion at Tara, existed in written sources. The incidental details in 1–10 and their naïvety are consistent with oral tales. The fact that miracle 6, 'Grazacham or the Founding of Armagh', is more highly developed than the others is explained by Muirchú's project – the promotion of Armagh's pre-eminence.

Even in Muirchú's time there was controversy over the burial place of Saint Patrick. Archaeologists have ventured the opinion that in order to prevent a pagan-style cult of the dead growing up around his tomb, Patrick asked for its location to be kept a secret. It was not revealed until Colmcille had a vision telling him to inform the world that Patrick was buried at Downpatrick. Miracle 14, 'Untamed Oxen Choose Burial Place', is a convenient way of implying that Patrick did not dismiss the all-important Armagh as a burial place, by taking the matter out of his hands entirely.

Unlike Muirchú, Tírechán was not trying to construct a narrative life of Saint Patrick. His book is an account of Patrick's travels in Meath and Connaught.

Tírechán was a disciple of Ultán, bishop of Ardbraccan, Co. Meath, who furnished him with both written and oral tradition about Patrick. Ultán, like Muirchú's patron Bishop Aedh, was, it will be remembered, old enough to be an important source of early oral tradition: like Muirchú, what Tírechán is setting down is tradition informed by a certain authority, but consisting of stories which had doubtless been 'improved' (or distorted) in 150 years of the telling.

Tirechán is of less interest to the non-specialist reader because he is essentially compiling a list of churches founded by Patrick in Meath and Connaught, together with lists of bishops appointed, rivers crossed, wells prayed at and so on, in order to establish the extent of Patrick's parish so that Armagh could assert its jurisdiction over it. While local historians rejoice in discovering from Tirechán that Patrick apparently set foot on their patch, most people find this list of mainly obsolete place-names of little interest.

Tirechán has a short list of 'sayings' of Patrick at the start of his book which have attracted much scholarly interest over the years. The first of these, 'The fear of God I had as my guide through Gaul and Italy and the islands in the Tyrrhene Sea', is often cited as evidence that Patrick studied in Gaul. The second and third ('Thanks be to God') are uncontentious. The fourth recommends the daily use of 'Kyrie eleison, Christe eleison, Kyrie eleison'. For liturgical reasons it is now believed to be a later addition to the Patrick canon – a way of making the saint appear to endorse a recently introduced element of liturgy. The 'Kyrie eleison' was first introduced into the western Church by Pope Gelasius I (492–6), at least 30 years after the 'official' date – 461 – of Patrick's death, and not even in time to reach him had he died in 492.

Even though there is little characterization in Tirechán's account of Patrick, he shares the same tendency as Muirchú's Patrick to curse those who cross him. He also makes a start on a habit he will develop in later *Lives* of blessing certain rivers that they may abound in fish, and cursing other rivers to sterility if the fishermen have not acceded to his request for fish to eat.

Tirechán frequently mentions that after Patrick has made a convert and established a foundation he then makes an alphabet for the convert. It has often been suggested that one reason why Ireland took so readily to the new religion was that, along with the mysteries of Christianity, converts were also initiated into the art of writing, a skill which no one in pagan Ireland (apart from those using the clumsy ogham script) had mastered. To the native Irish, with their love of poetry and saga, the ease with which the Christian wrote down his tales must have seemed, in itself, little short of miraculous.

Patrick, in his travels as related by Tirechán, is frequently challenged by hostile druids. One does get a sense of menace, tradition's version of the dangers that the historical Patricius tells us he confronted daily, though in the traditional version danger is always quickly averted by some display of miraculous power.

Tirechán's Patrick is especially assiduous in appropriating those wells which the druids worshipped and re-dedicating them to Christianity, a technique used by missionaries the world over, and one which has its repercussions in the practice of Christianity to this very day.

The historical association of Saint Patrick with particular places in Ireland originated with Muirchú and Tirechán. Their work was added to and embroidered by subsequent hagiographers, but they were using the same traditional legends. Lack of firm historical evidence associating Saint Patrick with certain places has not diminished their popularity. Most people continue to believe, and it is still taught in primary schools, that Saint Patrick spent six years of captivity on Mount Slemish, in Co. Antrim, herding Miliucc's flocks. There is, of course, no harm in retaining traditional beliefs, particularly if they help to bring the saint to life for the young, but Slemish, it must be admitted, is not the most impressive of the places made famous by the saint.

Slemish, which I am told is pronounced to rhyme with 'Flemish', is about fifteen miles inland from the beautiful coast road of the Glens of Antrim. The nearest town is Broughshane, a small farming community. Slemish is visible for miles around, its distinctive bulbous shape rising 1437 feet in a lump out of the landscape. To approach it one drives up the foothills, through pleasantly underpopulated arable farmlands along tiny lanes where dog roses and honeysuckle grow wild in the tall hedges. The car park is half-way up the mount, and from there, the rest of it looks disappointingly small. The car park, with its picnic tables and public toilets, is designed more for a family outing than for pilgrims in search of Saint Patrick. There is no statue of the saint, no plaque explaining his association with the place, not even a simple cross. The climb to the top of Slemish takes about ten minutes. The reward is a stunning view of the surrounding countryside, with the town of Ballymena in the distance, and, on almost any day of the year, a blast of icy wind. It is a bleak, exposed spot, and could have been designed for training saints in ascetic practices. But if the young Patrick was there as a swineherd he would not have spent much time on its summit because there is no vegetation there for an animal to graze on. He would have been working in the sheltered foothills.

'Saint Patrick's Footmark', the footprint in a stone mentioned by Muirchú is not in fact at Slemish, but at Skerry Church in nearby Magheramully. The footprint is believed to have been left by the Angel Victor when he ascended back to heaven after visiting Saint Patrick. Skerry Church is believed to occupy the site of the home of Patrick's owner, Miliucc. Not many people bother to make the detour there from Slemish.

Slemish is a pleasant enough place to visit, but nothing about it helped to convince me that this was the place where Patrick spent six years as a slave. This partly intuitive reaction, I found, emerged strongly for or against an association with the saint at each site I visited. I prefer a Connaught location for Saint Patrick's slavery – somewhere in Co. Mayo, perhaps even the foothills of Croaghpatrick. That would explain why he had to travel 200 miles to take the ship when escaping from Ireland – a plausible distance if crossing from the west coast to an east coast port, but a hard distance to explain if travelling from Slemish to one of the many ports on the nearby coast of Antrim. A Connaught location would also explain why, later in life, when the 'voice of the Irish' came to him in a dream, he identified them as being 'those beside the Wood of Voclut, which is near the Western Sea'.

Some thirty miles south of Slemish is the Lecale peninsula, an area far richer in traditional associations with the saint, but far less famous than Slemish. The place most strongly associated with the saint in Lecale is the tiny hamlet called Saul.

Although Downpatrick, a market town two miles from Saul, is

the traditional burial place of Saint Patrick – the 'Dun Lethglaisse' mentioned first by Muirchú (Miracle no. 14) to which the yoked oxen bore the saint's body – Saul has much stronger associations with the saint, a fact nowadays graciously conceded by the people of Downpatrick. These associations are carefully fostered by both the local Catholic and Protestant communities and the tourist department. They arise from the traditional belief that Dichu, Patrick's first convert, lived at Saul and gave Patrick the barn (*sabhall*) in which Ireland's first Christians worshipped. Patrick often returned to Saul, a place for which he had a great affection, to rest between his journeys. It was here that he died on 17 March 461 (see Muirchú, no. 12) and here that he was waked (see Muirchú, no. 13). According to the eighth-century 'Hymn of Saint Fiacc', Patrick received his last communion from Saint Tassach, Bishop of Raholp, a neighbouring hamlet.

Saul is situated at the base of a range of low hills which have a fine view of Strangford Lough and its several islands. A church was built on top of these hills in 1932 by the Church of Ireland to commemorate the 1500th anniversary of Saint Patrick's arrival in Ireland. It is a small, grey building with a conically-topped round tower, an imaginative but none-too-authentic replica of an early Irish church. It was built on the site of Saul Abbey, which was destroyed in 1316. The small interior is dimly lit by narrow slits at the side and a stained-glass triptych over the altar. The wooden beams of its vaulted ceiling add to the intimacy. All that remains of the old abbey is part of a wall and two corbelled anchorites' cells which stand in the graveyard of the new church. The cells command a fine view of the surrounding countryside.

At the bottom of the hill is the Catholic parish church of Saul. Here I found the first of many dubious relics of Saint Patrick. Behind the modern altar of this church is an old stone slab, about the size of a door, propped on its side, which is said to be 'a portion of the altar stone used by Saint Patrick'. Pilgrims touch it reverently with the palm of their hand as they file past. Who is to say it is *not* part of Saint Patrick's altar stone? Whether it is or not, it is a good piece of stone, uniquely weathered by the hands of generations of pilgrims. It is hard to resist the impulse to give it a rub for luck.

Understandably, the church does not advertise the story behind Saint Patrick's altar stone. It is one of many far-fetched tales about Saint Patrick that entered into folklore and remained in the repertoire of the *seanachies* (story-tellers working in the oral tradition) well into this century. There are several variations of the story. The one that I prefer has Saint Patrick returning to Ireland from a visit to Rome. When he went to take ship for the last leg of his journey, the captain told him that there was no room on board for the altar stone. The saint picked it up and threw it behind the boat, cursing the captain for his lack of co-operation. The stone floated, and Saint Patrick sat on top of it and was carried back to Ireland on it in the wake of the boat.

The year that celebrated the 1500th anniversary of Patrick's arrival in Ireland, 1932, was before the age of ecumenicism. The Church of Ireland built its replica church at Saul, and the Catholics erected 'a National and Catholic' monument on a neighbouring hill, which is now known as Slieve Patrick. It is a ten-metre tall statue of the saint in Mourne granite. He is wearing bishop's robes and mitre and has one hand raised in a blessing. It is a pleasant climb to the statue, and from the top of the hill there are more views of Strangford Lough and the surrounding countryside.

Less than a mile from Saul are the badly weathered remains of Raholp Church, where Saint Patrick is believed to have received the viaticum from Bishop Tassach. Only the walls remain. The decayed state reached by Raholp Church before it was rescued by archaeologists some 30 years ago – it was in the middle of a field grazed by cattle at the time – indicates the way that things might have gone if great efforts had not been made locally to preserve the area's Saint Patrick heritage. It is due to the hard work of enthusiastic archaeologists, amateur and professional, and an enlightened government policy, that there are so many well-tended, well-signposted sites to visit in the area. There are more sites to be excavated, but such work, I was told, has been postponed 'until things settle down'. In Lecale you feel a million miles away from the troubles, but Belfast is only twenty-five minutes up the road.

There are *raths*, stone circles, a motte, a cairn, churches, castles, wells, and in Downpatrick itself there is the cathedral, the remains of Inch Abbey, and a small museum called the Saint Patrick Heritage Centre. One of the strangest sites in the area is Struell Wells, a series of bath-houses built over a stream, known as the River Slán ('health' in Irish), in a small green valley on the outskirts of Downpatrick. I visited them in the company of Albert W. K. Colmer, one of the archaeologists responsible for the excavation and preservation of the Lecale peninsula, and could not have asked for a more knowledgeable guide.

The Wells were supposedly blessed by Saint Patrick during his travels: like Saul, they occupy a site to which the saint often returned to rest. Albert pointed to a spot known as Saint Patrick's Seat, a rocky throne high above the Wells, where the saint used to sit and contemplate. So strong is the eerie atmosphere of the place that for a moment one could easily believe that Saint Patrick had been there – not the elderly bishop of the popular image but, as Albert said, 'a youngish man in Roman sandals and a rough hair shirt with maybe a pigskin over the top to keep him dry and warm'.

Yet at the same time there is a strong residue of paganism to be experienced at Struell Wells. Perhaps it comes from the odd way that the site is marked out by stone walls, with small corbelled stone huts above the individual wells and two partially ruined larger bath-houses. It is a mysterious place, in which sounds echo, and it feels totally isolated in spite of its proximity to the outskirts of Downpatrick. There is little doubt that the tradition of the curative properties of the Wells predates its associations with Saint Patrick. Albert Colmer said that the Slán has the highest mineral content of any river in the area. In Christian times the place was visited on Saint John's Eve, 23 June, which is also Midsummer's Eve – a date closely associated with pagan celebrations. People went there to do penance and to seek cures. Pilgrims climbed the hill to Saint Patrick's Seat on their knees (not an easy climb, even on your feet) and circled his seat seven times, still on their knees, while reciting the prescribed prayers. There are records of 'vast crowds' gathering at Struell Wells on Saint John's Eve and the Friday before Lammas (1 August) throughout the eighteenth and early nineteenth centuries, 'some in hopes of obtaining health and others to perform penances'. The same 1898 guidebook continues: 'Disturbances having occurred here on several occasions early in the present century, the Roman Catholic clergy discouraged these practices, and the place is now quite deserted.'[5]

The events at Struell Wells were duplicated many times over throughout Ireland in the nineteenth and early twentieth centuries, as the clergy attempted to bring their flock under the control of post-Tridentine Catholic convention, and eliminate practices which they deemed to have a pagan origin. Many of these practices had by then become associated with Saint Patrick or some other native saint, but still the clergy mistrusted them. It was beyond the power of the church to control the behaviour which took place at such assemblies so, in many cases, instead of attempting to Christianize customs which had retained their pagan characteristics in spite of some 1300 years of Christianity, the church condemned them from the pulpit and did everything possible to discourage their continuance.

Visitors to Struell Wells these days are mainly tourists, and also local kids and punks who enjoy congregating in that quiet spot along with (may Saint Patrick strike them dumb!) their ghetto-blasters. They were arriving as I left, presumably to join another group already assembled in a chosen corner, to spend the after-noon showing off for the tourists' cameras.

And yet there are many people alive who can recall pilgrims seeking cures at Struell in the 1930s, among them Canon Joseph Maguire, the parish priest of Downpatrick. 'The tradition was kept alive by the people,' he told me. 'I have no knowledge of clergy participation or ceremonies of any kind, but I know that the local historical society, mainly priests, were very much involved and concerned about the restoration of the place. It is a beautiful spot which I often visit, and to which I bring all my visitors. One feels in touch with the poor of the past on those crude stone benches.'

3

THE *TRIPARTITE LIFE*
AND CROAGHPATRICK

Between the *Lives* of Muirchú and Tirechán and the next important *Life* of Saint Patrick there is another gap of some 200 years.
The *Tripartite Life* (or *Bethu Phátraic*) is the first extant *Life* of
Patrick written in Irish. It was composed *c.* 895–901, although
the manuscripts from which it has been reconstructed mostly
date from the fifteenth century. It was designed to be read as a
sermon, or to provide material for sermons to be preached during
the three-day celebration (*triduum*) which started on 16 March,
and was in honour of the day to which Saint Patrick's death is
traditionally assigned – 17 March.

It seems that the feast of Patrick's 'falling asleep' was well and
truly institutionalized by the early ninth century – and possibly
for long before that. A note in the *Book of Armagh* (*c.* 807) directed
that all monasteries and churches of Ireland should honour
the memory of Patrick's death by 'the celebration, during three
days and three nights in mid-spring, with every kind of good
food except flesh, of the festival of his "falling asleep".' The
prohibition on meat is because 17 March always falls during
Lent.

Just how far removed the early medieval celebration of Saint
Patrick's Day was from the largely secular and increasingly jocular modern celebrations can be seen by taking a look at the *Tripartite Life*. It is divided into three separate and lengthy homilies
which could either be read to the community or used as the basis
for sermons stressing local Patrician lore or whatever aspect of
Patrick's life appealed to the community in question. The first
sermon has some kind of structural unity; the other two have
none: a homiletical introduction and conclusion enclose a string
of Patrician anecdotes often lacking even the crudest form of

geographical coherence. Although ninety per cent of the text is in Irish, lengthy passages in Latin are interspersed.

Perhaps the most striking feature of the *Tripartite Life* is its continuation of the process of recasting Patrick in the mould of an Irish epic hero. Muirchú and Tirechán were writing during that period which is often referred to as the 'Golden Age' of Irish Christianity. Much has been written of the achievements of the Irish church in the sixth and seventh centuries, the learning and asceticism of its monks, and the important part they played in revitalizing continental Christianity. But we have already seen, in the work of Muirchú and Tirechán, that the early Irish church was stongly characterized by certain elements which it had absorbed from the native society. It was more of an Irish church than a Roman one: there is no record of any written correspondence between the Pope and the leaders of the Irish church for over four centuries – from 640 to 1080. And, as we have seen, even in Muirchú's day at the height of the 'Golden Age' (*c.* 670–90), it was necessary to endow Saint Patrick with qualities more suited to a native secular hero than to a Christian saint.

The rapid growth of monastic settlements in the century following Patrick's death, and the accompanying establishment of thriving scriptoria, is in itself evidence to confirm the existence of Christianity in Ireland before the dates commonly associated with Patrick. Whether one takes 461 or 493 as the date of Patrick's death, it is remarkable, given the non-literate state of pagan Irish society, that by *c.* 550 distinctively Hiberno-Latin writings of high quality were being produced.

Irish monks of this period were renowned for their asceticism. 'No Western Christians were so distinguished for their ascetic practices as the Irish' writes Whitley Stokes, the first modern (1887) editor of the *Tripartite Life*:

Thus we read of Finnchu sleeping with corpses, and suspending himself on sickles inserted in his armpits; of Ultán keeping a stone in his mouth during the whole of Lent; of Ite allowing her side to be eaten away by a stag beetle; of Ciaran mixing his bread with sand . . .

*

Other practices mentioned by Stokes include fasting, retiring for a time to a cave, standing in cold water, and bouts of sustained repetitive prayer. All these practices were attributed to Saint Patrick by Muirchú and they continue to be stressed in the *Tripartite Life*. Sustained repetitive prayer remains a characteristic of Irish Catholicism, as does another practice initiated by Patrick and developed by the monks of the Golden Age: that of voluntary exile among heathens. This is, of course, at the root of the modern missionary movement, and it is the reason why Ireland's foremost missionary order took Saint Patrick as its patron.

We have seen how Patricius, in his own writings, considers his exile among the pagan Irish as a sacrifice on his part, a sacrifice rewarded by the conversion of the heathen, but nevertheless a self-imposed exile. The early Irish monks did not initially undertake voluntary exile in order to convert the heathen, but rather as the ultimate form of penance – the ultimate ascetic practice. When Saint Colmcille went to Iona in 563 he did not intend to found a foreign mission: he wanted to make the great sacrifice of leaving his beloved native land. But such was the desire of local heathens for conversion that he was forced to turn Iona into a mission. Columbanus sought exile around the year 590 and travelled to the Continent. At this time continental Christianity was in something of a decline, and Columbanus, and other monks like him, did much to revitalize it. Many Irish monks journeyed to the Continent in search of solitude, and instead found themselves helping the local inhabitants to establish monasteries on the ascetic Irish model.

Most of these monks travelled with a well-stocked book satchel, and these works produced in Irish scriptoria were greatly treasured. A service book from Bangor dating from the seventh century found its way to Bobbio in Italy, probably carried there by a pilgrim monk. Along with their books, this first wave of Irish emigrants carried with them their devotion to Saint Patrick. Early texts and later copies of Hiberno-Latin texts have been discovered all over continental Europe in the past hundred years. These pilgrim monks were the first of many waves of Irish exiles to carry their devotion to Saint Patrick abroad, helping to turn the national apostle into an internationally venerated cult figure.

The evidence of the *Tripartite Life* points to an increase, rather than a slackening off, in the influence of the old native order on the Irish church. There is other evidence for the influence of native traditions and social organization on the Irish church. Patrick's effort to establish the Roman ecclesiastical system of dioceses and bishops was never very successful. Because monasteries were so important, abbots tended to wield more power than bishops who were often subordinate to their local abbot, superior only in their licence to ordain priests. Abbacies soon became hereditary, handed down from one member of the family to another along with their wealth and status.

In fact, the famous Golden Age of Irish Christianity was relatively short-lived. By the eighth century the ascetic life of the fifth and sixth centuries had given way to a far more comfortable one. Vows of poverty and chastity were no longer strictly observed. Within the hierarchy of society, priests and monks enjoyed the same stature as nobles, and many of them lived like nobles, too. So far had Irish monastic life regressed from its ascetic beginnings that between *c.* 770 and 840 a drastic reform movement – the *Celé De* (Culdee) was initiated.

It was in the same era, in 795, that the first Viking raiders came to the coast of Ireland. The wealth of the monasteries was a major factor in attracting the invaders and ensuring their frequent return.

The Vikings were not the only problem that Ireland had to face in the eighth and ninth centuries. The common image of a peaceful land of saints and scholars practising the sort of Christianity that we would recognize today is a highly misleading one. By the eighth century there is evidence of widespread apostasy, and a largely nominal Christianity. Native culture and social mores were not as easy to eradicate as the early Christian missionaries had believed. Long before the first Viking raids, the wealthy monasteries were being attacked and plundered by native armies. The historian Kenneth Neil mentions some two dozen such attacks, and adds that 'among this total were several depredations by Feidlimid MacCrimthainn, a colourful king of Munster, who also happened to be Bishop of Cashel . . . clearly, even eighth-century Ireland was not the "Isle of Saints and

Scholars" so famous in popular legend.' More correctly, it was, in Neil's words, 'a fossilized, semi-Christian society on the verge of political collapse'.

In order to understand the continuing 'Gaelicization' of the Patrick legend evident in the *Tripartite Life*, it is essential to dismiss the idea of a homogenously Romanized Christian Ireland, and to appreciate the unique character which Irish Christianity had taken on by the early 900s. The very fact that almost all of the *Tripartite Life* is written in Irish is in itself very significant. It will be remembered that before the arrival of Christianity the only script known in Ireland was ogham. One imaginative authority has worked out that to write a modern novel of average length in ogham would take five miles of paper. Native scholars devised a way of using the Roman alphabet to write in the Irish language, and by the early seventh century native oral tradition was being transcribed in Irish monasteries alongside Latin biblical texts. Not unnaturally, the existence of a written language caused something of an intellectual renaissance in native culture. Indeed, the degree of tolerance that the native and the Latin worlds of learning held for each other as early as the seventh century is quite remarkable, and also quite at variance with the strictures of fifth- and sixth-century bishops, who took great pains to isolate their newly converted Christians from the ways of pagan society.

It is characteristic of the literary history of Saint Patrick (even to the present day) that as a new *Life* gains in popularity, earlier ones fall into disuse, are neglected and often lost. The *Tripartite Life*, written, as we have said, *c*. 895–901, is known to have been in existence in a manuscript (now lost) of 1477, indicating an unusually long lifespan. Another index of its popularity is that many of the Saint Patrick tales surviving in Irish-speaking oral tradition can be traced back to it.

The *Tripartite Life*, in an abridged form, remained for many centuries the most popular *Life* of Patrick for the Irish-speaking community. The Saint Patrick of the *Tripartite*, with a few minor additions, remained the dominant Saint Patrick for the Irish-speaking community up to the early decades of this century, with the stern, argumentative, quick-tempered version of Saint Patrick surviving into the twentieth-century oral folklore tradition.

James F. Kenney, in his standard work *The Sources for Early Irish History*, gives a succinct summary of the place and purpose of the *Tripartite Life*:

> The *Tripartite Life* shows the evolution of the Patrick Legend nearly completed. Only minor elaborations have since taken place. In general form and character – the topographical basis, the loose stringing together of material of the most miscellaneous kind and origin, the free way in which historical facts and personages, legendary heroes, place-names, tribal fortunes, proverbs, local folklore are all brought into association with the central theme – it resembles some of the later developments of the secular cycles of romances . . . It is based chiefly on Muirchú, Tirechán and the other Patrician documents transcribed or indexed in the *Book of Armagh*. The additions to these sources are for the most part of folkloric or mythopoeic character. But it is clear that behind the compilation as a whole lay the same ecclesiastical purpose as behind the work of Tirechán . . . and Ferdomnach [the scribe of the *Book of Armagh*] and those 'heirs of Patrick' to whom Ferdomnach makes reference [i.e. the hierarchy of Armagh].
>
> The compiler is careful to make note of all the churches founded by Patrick and his disciples, of all grants made to them, and of any special claims the saint has on the allegiance of particular peoples. He also occasionally notices cases where churches which in his opinion should form part of the *paruchia Patricii* have passed under the control of other ecclesiastical organizations.

The Patrick presented in the *Tripartite* is even more overbearing and ill-tempered than the Patrick of Muirchú. His actions are usually more consistent with a pagan epic hero than a Christian saint. When his sister Lupait, for example, commits a sin of lust with one Colman, Patrick, who is enraged, chastises her by running her over in his chariot not once, but three times, killing her stone dead. He is also much given to cursing.

The *Tripartite* contains Tirechán's topographical information on Patrick's travels, and his catalogue of conversions, ordinations and church foundations. Many more topographical details and genealogies are added, especially material relating to Munster (an area of Ireland not covered by Tirechán). The genealogies and the topographical references must have had resonances for a contemporary audience now lost to us: we can imagine the thrill of hearing that Patrick had set foot in or near our home base:

> Patrick went thereafter into Tír Cairedo, and founded at Ard Licce a church, namely, Sendomnach; and he left therein Deacon Coemán. And Patrick built Ard Senlis, where he placed holy Lallócc, and he obtained a place in Mag Nento. And they went with Bishop Cethech to his country. Of the race of Ailill was Cathech's mother.

There is much of this sort of thing in the *Tripartite Life*.

Patrick's genealogy has been upgraded. His mother, Concessa, is said to have been a kinswoman of Martin of Tours, linking him with the most prestigious and popular figure of continental monasticism.

A new set of miracles, commonly referred to as the childhood miracles, first appear in the *Tripartite*. They begin at Patrick's birth. The flagstone on which he was born pours forth water if anyone commits perjury on it. Ethnologists have found this miracle of interest for the light it sheds on childbirth in early Irish society – that it was apparently customary to give birth on a flagstone.

The child Patrick, while growing up in Britain, spends his childhood not with his natural parents, as was the British custom, but in fosterage, as was the custom among the Irish nobility. The childhood miracles are folk-tales, obviously imported from oral tradition. Such is the appeal of these tales in certain quarters that they survived in the repertoire of many *seanachies* until quite recent times.

Another tale from folklore which first appears in the *Tripartite Life* concerns Saint Patrick's staff, which, according to this story, had originally belonged to Jesus Christ, no less. Christ had prophesied that Patrick would come and preach to the Gael, and when Patrick fulfilled this prophecy, the *Baculus Jesu* was handed over to him. This is the staff which features in most pictorial representations of the saint. It was venerated in Ireland until the time of the Reformation, when it was destroyed.

It is in the *Tripartite* that the text of a prayer which has been associated ever since with Saint Patrick first appears. It is known variously as 'Saint Patrick's Breastplate', the 'Lorica of Saint Patrick' or 'The Deer's Cry'. The last name is given because it occurs in the *Tripartite* and many later *Lives* during the battle with Loegaire at Tara, when Patrick and his followers successfully evade capture and death by disguising themselves as deer.

'The Deer's Cry' is a remarkable piece of poetry by any standards. Unfortunately there is little likelihood that it was actually composed by Saint Patrick, as was once widely believed. Most modern scholars, including Thomas Kinsella, part of whose translation from the Irish is given below, assign it to the eighth century.

> Christ beside me,
>   Christ before me,
>   Christ behind me,
>
> Christ within me,
>   Christ beneath me,
>   Christ above me,
>
> Christ on my right hand,
>   Christ on my left,
>
> Christ where I lie,
>   Christ where I sit,
>   Christ where I rise,
>
> Christ in the hearts of all who think of me,
> Christ in the mouths of all who speak to me,
> Christ in every eye that sees me,
> Christ in every ear that hears me.
>
> Today I put on
> a terrible strength,

invoking the Trinity,
confessing the Three,
with faith in the One
as I face my Maker.

The major contribution made by the *Tripartite* to the Patrick legend is the Croaghpatrick story, whose legacy today is a pilgrimage to a mist-covered mountain-top in County Mayo still undertaken annually by tens of thousands of people.

Croaghpatrick is called Cruachan Aigil or the Reek in the *Tripartite*. In Tirechán, Saint Patrick's ordeal on Cruachan Aigil occupies one brief paragraph. This is expanded to the length of some four pages in the *Tripartite*. Patrick stayed on the mountain 'in much displeasure, without food, from Shrove Saturday to Easter Sunday, after the manner of Moses'. He was tormented by demons who assumed the form of black birds. He sang 'maledictive psalms' at them, rang his bell so loudly that 'the men of Ireland heard its voice', and finally threw the bell at the demons so hard that it broke, and the black birds departed. Then Patrick wept. An angel came to console him, and Patrick argued lengthily with the angel to secure special dispensations for the Irish people.

The belief that he also cast the snakes out of Ireland during his ordeal on Croaghpatrick originated in oral tradition sometime between the ninth century and the arrival of the Normans, who were the first of many to dismiss this belief as superstition. Nevertheless, the association of Saint Patrick with Ireland's lack of snakes remains strong to this day.

The tradition that Patrick spent forty days and forty nights fasting on Croaghpatrick during Lent before casting the demons out of Ireland has also survived the test of time. Today Croaghpatrick remains strongly associated with the saint, and its ascent is still regarded by many people as a form of penance. Some people are fulfilling a promise made to Saint Patrick that they would climb it in thanksgiving for some favour received. Many others, Irish and foreign tourists alike, climb Croaghpatrick for the sheer pleasure of the views.

Croaghpatrick, or the Reek, as it is called locally, was known as

Cruachan Aigil – the Mount of the Eagle – before it became associated with Saint Patrick. A massive, imposing mountain by Irish standards and, at 2150 feet, among the highest in Connaught, it is on the west coast of the Republic, rising above Clew Bay, a wide stretch of sea dotted with small islands and framed by mountain ranges. It seldom fails to impress the traveller. The novelist Thackeray was moved to superlatives by his first sight of Croaghpatrick: 'From an eminence I caught sight, not only of a fine view, but of the most beautiful, I think, I ever saw in the world. Clew Bay and the Reek which sweeps down to the sea with its hundred isles dressed up in purple and gold, and the whole cloudy west in a flame! Wonderful! Wonderful! It is a challenge and a reward to the climber.'

My first view of the strong, dark silhouette of Croaghpatrick came towards the end of a seven-hour cross-country drive, on the road between Castlebar and Westport. Its distant shape loomed up, unmistakable and menacing in the dusk, getting bigger and bigger as I got closer. The sight was a fitting finale to any journey.

I arrived on a Saturday evening in order to climb the Reek on Garland Sunday – or Garlick Sunday, as some old people still call it – the last Sunday in July, and now the traditional date for the ascent. Garland Sunday evolved from *Lughnasa*, a pagan festival marking the end of summer.

The tradition of climbing Croaghpatrick on Garland Sunday is first mentioned in 1432. Before that the people climbed it on the previous Friday – Garland Friday – and many of the more devout local people still do, to avoid the holiday atmosphere which develops on the Sunday. The earliest known records mention pilgrims climbing the Reek on Saint Patrick's Day. The *Annals of Loch Cé* record a thunderstorm on 17 March 1113, during which 30 pilgrims were killed on the summit. Other records complain of harsh weather met with during the ascent, and this, combined with the fatal thunderstorm of 1113, was probably responsible for the decision to move the pilgrimage from March to July.

The weekend of Garland Sunday is the busiest time of the year in Westport, the nearest town to the Reek. It is a remarkably unspoilt and pretty place with many Georgian buildings and small, old-fashioned shops. The best restaurants are down on the quay, and I managed to get a table at the Asgard Inn at about 10 o'clock. A loud and jovial foursome were leaving as I arrived.

'Are you climbing the Reek tomorrow?' the landlady asked them, smiling.

'I'm going up it now,' said a fat man, banging his fist on the counter.

'He's not fit to climb the stairs, let alone the Reek!' said his girlfriend, laughing at the very idea.

Nowadays the first Mass on the summit of the Reek is at 8 a.m. It used to be at six, and many people started climbing soon after midnight by the light of a torch. 'You could see the flashlights from here, going up the hill in a long line,' the landlady told me. 'They used to start climbing it after the pubs closed, it was just an excuse for a booze-up, so the bishops tried to put a stop to it, by moving the first Mass to 8. But some of them still do it. They start from the car park just beyond Old Campbells.'

I was planning to sleep in the car and start climbing at first light, so I headed off to the car park 'just beyond Old Campbells', which turned out, inevitably, to be a pub, the centre of the tiny village of Murrisk. Lights were still blazing from its windows at midnight and small groups were gathered in the forecourt wrapped up against the equally inevitable rain, inspecting piles of sticks. These turned out to be 'ash-plants', the famous pilgrims' staff, which is an essential part of Reek-climbing equipment. It is a sturdy heavy stick, cut to just below shoulder height, which enables the pilgrim to get a grip on the scree near the summit. They were on sale for a modest fifty pence each. In twos and threes, groups of well-oiled merrymakers disappeared along a path beside the pub into the blackness, their flashlights re-emerging some hundred yards later as pinpoints of light inter-mittently visible through the rain.

It was tempting to follow them, but as luck would have it, my flashlight was not working, and I had forgotten to bring an ade-quate waterproof. However, I did have a lightweight showerproof jacket, a sleeping bag and a flask of hot coffee, so I retired to the car to catch whatever sleep I could. That was not much. The crowds leaving the pub grew noisier and rowdier: by one o'clock more merrymakers were arriving in cars, banging doors and shouting encouragement to each other:

'Is there many gone up the Reek?'

'I'd say there's a few gone up all right.'

'Have you a naggin on you, boy?'

'No, but I've a six-pack.'

The rain was pelting down by 2 a.m., lashed about by a cyclonic wind that rocked the car on its suspension. Other people were trying to sleep in cars and vans, and more kept arriving. By 3 a.m. the car park – about the size of half a football pitch – was full. By 4.30 dawn was breaking and, like the people in the car next to me, I sat up in my sleeping bag and poured a cup of hot coffee.

The storm had blown itself out, leaving only a slight drizzle and the promise of clearer weather in the sky. With a thick sweater under my jacket, a tweed cap on my head and a pair of double-skinned walking boots, I decided I would probably survive the Reek. I handed over 50p to a child for an ash-plant and set off.

The path at the base of the mountain is easy enough, bare rock alternating with mud and gravel, not much of a slope, and ferns and heather on either side. People of all ages were going up singly and in twos and threes when I began the climb. The merrymakers of the night before were coming down, pale-faced in spite of their exertions, and very much the worse for wear. Empty bottles and cans littering the path left no doubt as to why.

Higher up, the ferns and heather alongside the path gave way to scrub. After a fairly steep section the path went downhill for a while, past a circular tarn, and changed from rock and gravel to a combination of loose stones and fixed boulders. Some people chose to climb in small groups. Others, whether in company or not, followed their own pace. I was slightly ahead of a family party travelling in single file consisting of grandmother, parents and two barefoot daughters in their early twenties, each with a rosary in the left hand and an ash-plant in the right. Whenever my pace was flagging I caught sight of two pairs of bare feet, mud

Above: The lack of any historical evidence that Saint Patrick spent six years as a young slave on Mount Slemish in County Antrim has not weakened the popularity of the tradition. Its bulbous shape rises 1,437 feet above the surrounding plain and is visible for miles around.

Below: Struell Wells, a series of bath houses built over the river Slan ('health' in Irish) on the outskirts of Downpatrick, is one of the strangest sites associated with the saint. There is little doubt that the belief in the Wells' curative properties pre-dates their asssociation with Saint Patrick. Many older people can remember pilgrims seeking cures at Struell Wells on Saint John's Eve – 23 June – which is also Midsummer's Eve, a date associated with pagan festivities.

Above: The Lecale Peninsula, some thirty miles south of Slemish in County Down, is far richer in traditional associations with the saint, but far less well-known. It is believed that Saint Patrick returned regularly to the tiny hamlet of Saul to rest after his travels. This statue of the saint in Mourne granite is ten metres tall. It was erected in 1932 at Slieve Patrick, a hill above Saul overlooking Strangford Lough, as the Catholic monument to mark the 1,500th anniversary of the saint's arrival in Ireland.

Above: In the pre-ecumenical days of 1932 the Church of Ireland built a separate monument on a neighbouring hill to celebrate the 1,500th anniversary of Saint Patrick's arrival in Ireland. The replica of an early Irish church at Saul is believed to be very close to the site of the barn (Sabhall/ Saul is Irish for barn) in which Saint Patrick established Ireland's first church.

Left: The tiny village of Murrisk at the base of Croaghpatrick takes on a festive air on Garland Sunday (the last in July). The pilgrimage is a popular family outing and there is a brisk trade in cheap souvenirs.

Above right: A shoulder-high stick known as an ash plant is essential for the pilgrim on Croaghpatrick, giving a firm grip on the scree, the final steep stretch of the climb, where loose boulders tumble in all directions at every step.

Below right: Some 25,000 people climb the Reek (as Croaghpatrick is known locally) every year on Garland Sunday. Both the clergy and the medical profession discourage barefoot climbers, but some still follow the old tradition. Barefoot climbers risk cuts deep enough to cause arterial bleeding, multiple lacerations and twisted ankles. Broken spines and fractured skulls are the most common injuries among the shod. For most people, however, the pilgrimage is a unique and enjoyable outing: a well-shod, reasonably fit person will reach the summit and return again to the base in about four hours, given clement weather.

Above: The remains of Inch Abbey, where the Cistercian monk, Jocelin, wrote his *Life* of Saint Patrick in the twelfth century, consist of little more than the east end of the Abbey church. However, they are charmingly situated on the banks of the river Quoile, and the foundations of the whole complex have been uncovered so that it is possible to trace the alterations made between the twelfth and the fifteenth centuries. It is one of several well-maintained sites of archaeological interest in the Downpatrick area.

Right: Although all the authorities agree that Saint Patrick is not buried beside Downpatrick Cathedral, there is a persistent stream of visitors to his 'grave'. The large granite slab that marks its supposed location was carved and placed there in 1900 to discourage the practice of removing a handful of earth from the site; so numerous were the pilgrims that there was fear that this custom would erode the hill on which the cathedral stands.

Above: The pilgrimage to Station Island survived centuries of persecution because the people insisted on going there to do penance in spite of threats and physical violence against them. Since this aerial view was taken in the early 1960s, further construction work has been undertaken to improve facilities using land reclaimed from the lake. At present about 30,000 pilgrims stay on the island for three days and two nights between 1 June and 15 August. As many as 1,300 people have been accommodated on this tiny island together, although the average number of people staying overnight is about 750.

Below: Although changes have been made to the accommodation on Lough Derg, the spiritual exercises of the pilgrimage have changed very little since the seventeenth century when this map was printed. The circular penitential beds – the foundations of beehive huts once used by anchorites – around which penitents make their *stations* can be clearly seen.

Right: In many ways these early twentieth century pilgrims are better equipped than their modern counterparts who make their stations clad in knee-length skirts or jeans and flimsy anoraks. But the modern pilgrim has access to a night shelter during the short breaks in the all-night vigil, the use of the impressive new Basilica, and the additional choice of black coffee and plain toast on the menu of the daily 'Lough Derg meal' which previously consisted only of black tea and oatcakes.

Below: The barefoot pilgrim recites 280 prayers during each of the nine stations to be made on Station Island. Four of the stations are held communally in the Basilica during the all-night vigil; the others are performed individually, in silent prayer, on these beds in the daytime. The stones are sharp and very slippery in wet weather. Kneeling, which is done twice at each bed, is even more painful than walking. If rain is persistent and heavy, the clergy offer pilgrims the option of saying their daytime stations communally inside the Basilica: not everyone takes it up, as some believe that the hardship endured on the beds is an essential part of their penance.

The Basilica of Saint Patrick is an architectural triumph in the Hiberno-Romanesque style. It was consecrated in 1931. The spacious interior is unadorned to encourage a penitential frame of mind, the only ornamentation being a magnificent set of stained glass windows by Harry Clarke depicting the Stations of the Cross.

Every batch of pilgrims to Station Island contains a wide cross-section of Irish society. Once on the island, a camaraderie quickly grows up between those who are to spend the all-night vigil together. On the third day the group will be ferried back to the mainland where they must wait until midnight for the first square meal in three long days.

oozing over raw pink toes, and my own well-shod feet fairly flew over the path in relief at their relative comfort.

For some of the climb I kept pace with a frail lady of about seventy, a veteran Reek-climber originally from Co. Mayo, now living in Dublin, who had come down with a coach party that left Dublin at midnight. She carried her own walking stick. The ash-plant, she said, was so heavy it would wear you out, and the roughness of it would give you blisters. She was right: the only blisters I got from climbing the Reek were on my hand where it rubbed against the stick's rough bark.

I mentioned my admiration for the barefoot ones behind us, but my friend was not impressed. 'In my mother's day,' she told me, 'they never wore shoes if they could help it. You'd be a fool to go climbing the Reek in your shoes, you'd only destroy them, and your feet along with them. It was easier for them to climb in their feet. Nowadays we're all used to shoes, only a fool would climb the Reek without them.' Nevertheless, I noticed that many people shared my admiration for the barefoot ones, and quickened their own pace at the sight. All the barefoot pilgrims attracted groups of followers, as if people found inspiration in them. I do not think it was just morbid curiosity. One young man even stopped to take his own shoes off and hang them around his neck by the laces before continuing his climb.

The practice has been discouraged from the pulpit, and there are noticeably fewer barefoot climbers these days than there were in the past. I saw only about fifty among the early morning climbers, and proportionately less as the day went on. The discouragement of this practice has provoked a sharp reaction, not from the pilgrims themselves, but from Dublin-based liberal elements who dislike the clergy interfering with such an old tradition. The same people condemn the clergy's efforts to discourage the midnight climb, efforts which, to judge from what I saw and heard, have not been very successful. The people continue to do what they and their fathers before them have always done.

The clergy, however, have the medical profession on their side, and in fact co-operate with it by posting warning notices in the porches of local churches advising people with heart conditions, or bronchial or asthmatic trouble, not to climb the Reek. The volunteers from the Order of Malta, who provide ambulance crews for the occasion, do not go up the mountain until 6 a.m. Barefoot climbers, they told me, often get cuts deep enough to cause arterial bleeding, and also suffer from multiple lacerations and twisted ankles. Broken spines and fractured skulls are the most common injuries among the shod.There has not been a death on the Reek for two years, and that one was, they said, purely accidental and not attributable to drunkenness or climbing barefoot.

There are three penitental stations to be observed on the Reek, one, a memorial to Saint Patrick's disciple Saint Benignus, just before the scree, and two more at the top of the hill. The majority of early morning climbers followed the traditional ritual of stopping to say the prescribed prayers at each spot.

The worst part of the climb is after the first station. The path disappears, so does all vegetation. On either side and in front and behind there is nothing but loose grey rocks, the smallest the size of a rugby ball, the rest boulders. This is also the steepest part of the climb. With every step forward the stones tumble in all directions, mostly downwards. Apart from proceeding on all fours (which some people do), the only way to progress is by sticking your ash-plant in the stones and pulling yourself up on it. Once you are on the scree all orientation disappears: there is no sense of how close the top is, nor how far back you have left terra firma. The only way to climb, as my elderly friend advised me, is one step at a time, looking neither backwards nor forwards, but only at the next place to put your stick and your foot. To add to the drama of this stretch of the climb, a thick mist was on us and at times we could see no further than about three yards in any direction. Figures drifted into visibility then, ghost-like, disappeared.

My companion was in some bronchial distress, inching her way up the scree, coughing and retching and taking sips from a bottle of holy water to ease herself. She stopped to rest, and I sat beside her on another boulder. 'Short of oxygen,' she explained between coughs. 'The ambulance men will be along with some in a minute.' I offered to go and look for them. 'Don't mind me, girl,' she said. 'We all have to do our own penance and this is mine. Off with you now, or you'll miss the first Mass.'

I did as I was told. Shortly after, an ambulance crew emerged from the mist, not dispensing oxygen, but carrying down a stretcher case, an unconscious young man, blood seeping through the bandages on his head. Six volunteers carried the stretcher, and, because of the gradient, it was steadied by a further six men pulling on a loop of rope behind it.

Just when I started to believe that the scree was going to go on forever, I arrived at the summit. It was flat and circular and was already crowded with about 400 pilgrims. Some were making their station at Saint Patrick's Bed (a pile of rocks enclosed by a rectangle of low metal poles like a grave), some were standing in front of the oratory waiting for the first Mass, some were kneeling together to say a family rosary and others were sitting on large boulders, resting. I joined the latter group. The first thing everyone seemed to do after making their station, was to sit down and smoke a cigarette. Most people climb the Reek fasting, and the sandwiches must wait until after Mass. The climb had taken just over two hours. Shortly before the Mass started I was relieved to see my elderly friend with the bronchial trouble kneeling at Saint Patrick's bed, completing her annual pilgrimage. Penance or no penance, I felt guilty about abandoning her.

The 'oratory' is a bizarre and primitive building, undistinguished by anything other than its location. The priest, installed in a glassed-in box which protrudes from the front of it, says Mass over a loudspeaker to the crowd standing in the open air continually from 8 a.m. to noon. A door on the left is labelled 'Confession' and on the right 'Communion'. The interior consists of two wide corridors, and after kneeling on a wooden rail to receive communion, the pilgrim exits by the back door.

The oratory, and the continuing clerical involvement in the Garland Sunday pilgrimage, are a legacy of John Healy, Archbishop of Tuam, one of Saint Patrick's many nineteenth-century biographers. When he was appointed to the archbishopric in 1903, the annual pilgrimage had 'the character of a circumspect local gathering' (consisting, one assumes, largely of merrymakers). Healy's predecessor in the archbishopric had petitioned the Pope for permission to move the pilgrimage to a more accessible site, as he felt that the climb to the summit of the Reek was an excessive demand to make of his flock. Healy energetically set about restoring the pilgrimage to its traditional site, and rebuilding the oratory at its summit, which had been allowed to fall into ruins.

The problems associated with building on such an inaccessible site were overcome by the co-operation of the pilgrims themselves. Bags of cement and other materials packed in portable quantities were left at the base of the Reek, and pilgrims considered it such a privilege to carry materials to the summit that some made more than one ascent of the mountain in order to do so. The oratory was completed within a year and dedicated on 30 July 1905.

On my visit to the oratory the mist swirled around the waiting crowd, which included, as all Irish crowds do, several stray dogs. There was no sign, however, of the black birds who had tormented Saint Patrick on the Reek. The voice of a priest recently returned from 24 years in a Korean mission came over the loudspeaker system, saying what an honour it was for him to be invited to say the first Mass on the summit of this holy mountain and inviting us to join with him in Saint Patrick's prayer. It all seemed superfluous. The presence of Patricius is strong on top of the Reek, and next time I shall choose an ordinary weekday dawn to make the climb, in search of the solitude that Patricius experienced there.

Some elderly people can remember setting out on foot or by bicycle from as far afield as Dublin (over 162 miles away) to climb the Reek. Today they come by car and specially chartered coaches. In 1980, the year after the Pope's visit, some 60,000 pilgrims climbed the Reek on Garland Sunday. In 1986 the Garda estimated the crowd at about 25,000.

Pilgrims were streaming up the mountain as those who had attended the first Mass were coming down. The rain and mist had lifted, and the sun had come out. Once we were below the cloud that had settled on the summit there was a perfect view of Clew Bay and the surrounding countryside. We could see for miles – islands in a rough blue sea ahead, and on either side stretches of brown bogland with small dark blue lakes and vast expanses of bright green ferns. Some brave entrepreneurs had set

up stalls selling soft drinks, sweets and cigarettes close to the
summit. The pack-donkeys, who had hauled the stuff up, were
tethered nearby. A collie-type mongrel picked me up on the summit and followed at my heels the whole way down. It was, as I
had feared, almost more difficult to climb down the scree than it
had been to climb up. Groups of men were linking hands and
arms in a most un-Irish fashion to help each other along. We
formed one of the best-tempered crowds I have ever been part of.
'Not far to go now,' 'You'll be up there before you know it,' we
shouted encouragingly but mendaciously to those who were just
setting foot on the first of the scree. My companions were of all
ages. Accents from all parts of Ireland and England could be
heard, but the dominant element among the great mix was, to
judge by their unmistakable appearance, drawn from the ranks
of small farmers and their families.

I was back at the base by 9.30, and already experiencing a feeling of achievement and satisfaction that was to last for weeks.
Climbing the Reek is one of the most memorable ways to spend a
morning that I know of. As time went on, the atmosphere in the
car park became increasingly festive. The price of ash-plants
doubled to a hardly extortionate £1. The pub had been open since
8 a.m. and two chip vans were doing great business. The
approach to the Reek was lined with vendors of inexpensive religious trinkets and souvenirs. A hustler was selling his 'official
guide book for pilgrims' over a loudhailer – 'the nearest thing to a
magic carpet' – for a mere ten pence. It turned out to be a cheaply
printed sheet of paper giving perfectly correct instructions for
making the 'stations'. Saint Patrick was for sale in 1001 different
gaudy frames and settings, but the most remarkable feature of
these souvenirs was that every single one of them used exactly
the same picture of Saint Patrick: a patriarchal bishop in long
green vestments with a jewelled mitre and crozier, standing on a
rock and pointing to the serpents at his feet, with a cluster of
round towers behind his right elbow.

I hung around the base of Croaghpatrick watching pilgrims
arriving and looking at the brightly coloured ribbon of tiny figures which stretched all the way along the path of the Reek. I was
chatting to a Garda sergeant in the car park when a group of

youths carrying a large cassette player and wearing badges proclaiming 'I prayed for you on the Reek' passed us by. 'We call them pilgrims, but a lot of them are only here for the crack,' said the sergeant. Murrisk was crowded out, and everyone was enjoying the holiday atmosphere in their own particular way.

4
THE NORMAN VIEW
AND DOWNPATRICK

Within less than a hundred years of their first Irish raid in 795 the Vikings were establishing permanent settlements, centres of population which were to become the modern cities of Dublin, Wexford, Waterford, Cork and Limerick. By the year of the Battle of Clontarf – 1014 – they were well-established residents who had exerted a considerable influence on the native Irish, introducing a market economy and, through the new ports, opening Ireland up to the outside world. In their turn, the Vikings had adopted many native Irish ways, including Christianity.

This was not achieved, of course, without much upheaval. The Viking invaders waged merciless war on the Irish kings in their quest for land and loot. The Irish soon learned to apply Viking ruthlessness to their own inter-tribal battles, and the old Gaelic order fell into disarray. The rise of an obscure Munster chieftain, Brian Ború, to the High-Kingship of Ireland, is usually seen nowadays as having happened largely because of the decayed state of tribal Irish society.

The church was not spared the ravages of war. Ecclesiastical centres were invaded, sacked and plundered by both native factions and Vikings. It is impossible to know exactly how many manuscripts perished during these protracted wars, but some scholars believe that among them, 60 or 70 *Lives* of Saint Patrick were lost. Whether or not that is the case, there is another gap of over 200 years between the *Tripartite Life* of Saint Patrick (*c.* 895–901) and the next important *Life*, that of Jocelin, which was written in 1185 shortly after the Norman invasion.

The *Tripartite Life* was still in use at this period. No new *Life* seems to have emerged during the tentative peace which was established during the High-Kingship of Brian Ború, but this can

71

perhaps be explained by the decadent state of monastic life at the time. However, the pro-Armagh propaganda which permeated the works of Muirchú, Tirechán and the *Tripartite's* compiler, had the desired effect. When Brian Ború had finally forced the northern kings (with the exception of Tir Chonaill) to recognize him as High King, he proved his strength by going to Armagh, the ecclesiastical capital, to present himself in its church as *Imperator Scottorum* – 'Emperor of the Irish' – and depositing twenty ounces of gold on the altar to confirm formally the ecclesiastical supremacy of the apostolic see of Saint Patrick over the whole of Ireland. His scribe recorded the historic moment in the *Book of Armagh* in the presence of the High King, concluding his entry: 'I, Máel Suthain, have written this in the presence of Brian, emperor of the Irish, and what I have written he has determined for all the Kings of Cashel.'

Not everybody, however, agreed with Brian Ború. One indication of just how disorganized the native Irish church had become by the eleventh century is the fact that the first bishops of the now Christian Norse settlements based in the emerging cities, although Irish-born, chose to acknowledge the supremacy of Canterbury rather than that of Armagh. This was in order to avoid the system of hereditary abbacies and bishoprics which was endemic in the Irish church. Thus already, long before the sixteenth-century Reformation, there is evidence of a split within the Irish church, with the old stock of the rural areas giving their allegiance to Armagh, and the urban newcomers preferring to defer to Canterbury.

Although there is no record of formal written contact between Armagh and Rome between 640 and 1080, there was a certain amount of personal contact, through a string of Irish pilgrims. In 1028, for example, Sitric Silkbeard, King of Dublin, and Flannacán, King of Brega, went on a pilgrimage to Rome. Ecclesiastics also had contact with continental reformers who were reorganizing their own corrupt monasticism. Kings and ecclesiastics both saw the need to apply such measures to Irish monasteries and also to provide the country with a diocesan organization.

Foremost among the reformers was Saint Malachy who travelled several times to Rome as the representative of the Irish bishops. His contacts led to the introduction of continental monastic orders into Ireland. By 1126 there were Canons Regular of Saint Augustine in Armagh, the Benedictines arrived at around the same time and in 1142 the first Cistercians came to Mellifont.

There is controversy among historians as to just how effective the ecclesiastical reforms of the eleventh century were. Pope Hadrian IV, according to one school of thought, did not have much confidence in the ability of the Irish to reorganize their church. Either that, or he was misled by exaggerated reports from Irish pilgrims. Whatever the reason, in 1156 he gave permission for King Henry II to invade and conquer Ireland in the hope that the presence of Henry's people would help in the reform and reorganization of the Irish church. This papal initiative was not without precedent: 90 years before, Pope Alexander II had authorized William the Conqueror's invasion of England for similar reasons.

Henry, however, had other problems to contend with, and it was not until he was approached by one Diarmuid MacMurrough some ten years later that he decided to act on the Pope's authority. Diarmuid had been deposed as King of Leinster in 1166 by the King of Connaught. In 1167 he visited Henry in Aquitaine and offered to promote the Norman cause in Ireland in return for Henry's help in regaining his lands.

The conquest of Ireland was swift and efficient. So successful were the Earl of Pembroke (known as 'Strongbow') and his band of Norman warriors that by 1171, Henry himself found it necessary to visit Ireland in person to receive the allegiance of his new subjects in order to ensure that his barons did not set up an independent kingdom outside his authority.

One of the most outstanding features of the Norman conquest of Ireland was the rapidity with which the newcomers not only assimilated themselves into Irish society, but did so from the top, dominating the whole scene within a very short space of time.

To understand just how different these 'Normans' (most of the barons had previously been living in Wales, and they brought Flemish footsoldiers with them) were from the native Irish, we need only look at the work of Giraldus Cambrensis – Gerald of Wales. Giraldus came to Ireland in the course of his ecclesiastical career. His brother and uncle were among the first wave of invaders, and on his first visit to Ireland in 1183 he helped and advised them. Because of this he was considered an authority on Ireland at the Norman court, and in 1185 he was sent to accompany Henry II's youngest son John on his visit to Ireland. He stayed on after the royal visit to write a report on the state of the newly conquered land. The result is *The History and Topography of Ireland*, a fascinating if sometimes repugnant document.

Giraldus has a good gift for story-telling and a lively, opinionated style. But he is a controversial figure, gullible, vain and full of contempt for the Irish. His work marks the start of a tendency which can still be observed today, and was especially strong in the nineteenth century, of writing about the Irish people as a barbarous, uncouth, ill-tempered race of cretins.

Geoffrey Keating (*c.* 1570–1650), one of many historians who have endeavoured to undo the damage done by Giraldus, complains of the Welshman's pernicious influence: 'Everyone of the new Galls who writes on Ireland writes . . . in imitation of Cambrensis . . . because it is Cambrensis who is as the bull of the herd for them writing the false history of Ireland, wherefore they had no choice of guide.'

Here are two typical examples of Giraldus on the Irish: 'They are a wild and inhospitable people. They live on beasts only and live like beasts. They have not progressed at all from the primitive habits of pastoral living . . .' 'The people is, then, a barbarous people, literally barbarous. Judged according to modern ideas, they are uncultivated, not only in the external appearance of their dress, but also in their flowing hair and beards. All their habits are the habits of barbarians.' He comments quite early on in the *Topography* on the vindictiveness of Irish saints, a quality we have already observed in the early *Lives* of Saint Patrick, but not before making another unflattering generalization about the newly conquered race: 'This seems to me a thing to be noticed that just as the men of this country are during this mortal life more prone to anger and revenge than any other race, so in eternal death the saints of this land that have been elevated by their merits are more vindictive than the saints of any other region.'

Giraldus, during his description of the peculiarities of the Irish flora and fauna, is the first to mention of the legend that Saint Patrick banished the snakes and reptiles from Ireland. However, in an unusual bout of scepticism, the normally credulous Giraldus professes to doubt this 'pleasant conjecture'.

Of all kinds of reptiles only those that are not harmful are found in Ireland. It has no poisonous reptiles. It has no serpents or snakes, toads or frogs, tortoises or scorpions. It has no dragons. It has, however, spiders, leeches and lizards – but they are entirely harmless.

Some indulge the pleasant conjecture that Saint Patrick and other saints of the land purged the island of all harmful animals. But it is more probable that from the earliest times, and long before the laying of the foundations of the Faith, the island was naturally without these as well as other things.

Giraldus boasted to one admirer that he had made no use of earlier commentators or hagiographers in his account of Ireland. If that is true, it indicates that by 1185 the story of Patrick's banishing of the serpents was an accepted piece of oral tradition.

The ancients were well aware that Ireland had no snakes, but that knowledge had obviously ceased to be common currency by this time, both in the continental European tradition as represented by Giraldus, who, for all his shortcomings, must be considered well-educated by the standards of his day, and among the Irish people themselves. The earliest reference to Ireland's lack of snakes is made in the third century AD by the grammarian Gaius Julius Solinus: 'In that land there are no snakes, birds are few, and the people are inhospitable and warlike.'

There is a theory which suggests that the legend of the expulsion of the snakes is not of Irish origin, but Norse, and is based on a confusion between the Norse word for toad-expeller (*Pad-rekr*) and the Irish form of Patricius (*Padraig*). That the association between Patrick and snakes cannot be traced before the establishment of Viking settlements in Ireland would seem to support the notion.

Giraldus's description of Patrick is one of the few uncontroversial sections of his *Topography*:

> Patrick, Britannic by birth, a man distinguished for his life and holiness, arrived in this island, and, finding the people given to idolatry and deluded by various errors, was the first by the aid of divine grace, to preach and plant there the Christian faith. He baptized the people, whole crowds at a time, and, the entire island having been converted to the Faith of Christ, chose Armagh as his see. He made this place a kind of metropolis and special seat for the primacy of the whole of Ireland. He also appointed bishops in suitable places, so that, having been called to share his responsibility, they should water what he had planted.

But, in spite of the fact that Patrick converted 'the entire island' to the faith, Giraldus does not see much evidence of its practice at his time of writing. The next but one section, entitled 'The Irish are ignorant of the rudiments of the Faith' shows just how strongly pre-Christian practices persisted beneath a merely nominal adherence to Christianity among large sectors of the population. Even allowing for Giraldus's customary tendency to exaggeration, Pope Hadrian IV was perhaps correct in being concerned about the state of Irish Christians:

> Although since the time of Patrick and through so many years the Faith has been founded in the island, and has almost continuously thrived, it is, nevertheless, remarkable that this people even still remains so uninstructed in its rudiments.
>
> This is a filthy people, wallowing in vice. Of all peoples it is the least instructed in the rudiments of the Faith. They do not yet pay tithes or first fruits or contract marriages. They do not avoid incest. They do not attend God's church with due reverence. Moreover, and this is surely a detestable thing, and contrary not only to the Faith but to any feeling of honour – men in many places in Ireland, I shall not say marry, but rather

debauch, the wives of their dead brothers. They abuse them in having such evil and incestuous relations with them.

Giraldus is also the first person to mention the location of Patrick's tomb. Neither Muirchú nor Tirechán assigned a specific location to Patrick's burial place, and the *Tripartite Life* stated that one of the reasons why Patrick resembled Moses was that both their burial places were unknown. In the intervening years, however, a tradition appeared which asserted that Brigid, Colmcille and Patrick were all buried in Down: 'They were found there in our times . . . in a cave that had three sections. Patrick was lying in the middle, and the others were lying on either side. John de Courci, who was in command there, took charge when these three noble treasures were, through divine revelation, found and translated.'

John de Courcy was one of the most successful Norman adventurers to invade and plunder Ireland. He arrived in Ireland in 1177 with a force of 300 men and headed north to Ulster. At that time Downpatrick was the seat of Rory MacDonlevy, King of Ulster. De Courcy took his stronghold by surprise, and MacDonlevy's attempt to recover it was crushed, resulting in heavy losses. Within a mere six months, de Courcy was recognized as the most powerful king in Ulster.

Most historians attribute a political motive to de Courcy's claim to have discovered the relics of Saints Patrick, Brigid and Colmcille, because de Courcy used the discovery as an excuse to transfer the see of the diocese from Bangor to Down. At the same time he replaced the Irish Augustinians at Down with English monks from Chester. Among those English monks was Jocelin, a Cistercian from the monastery of Furness in Lancashire, whom de Courcy had chosen for a specific task: to write a *Life* that would raise Saint Patrick's standing among Ireland's new Norman rulers. The work was commissioned to enhance the prestige of the newly elevated see of Down, just as the *Tripartite* had continued the work of furthering the interests of Armagh.

Jocelin's *Life* is the first 'Anglicization' (or de-Gaelicization) of the Patrick legend. The *Tripartite Life*, written in Irish, and presenting Saint Patrick as an Irish hero, remained popular among Irish-speakers up to the mid-nineteenth century, while Jocelin's Patrick, a more conventional saint in the continental mode, defined Saint Patrick for those who read Latin or English in the same period.

Not much is known about the Monk of Furness. His best-known work is his *Life* of Saint Patrick. He also compiled the *Life and Miracles of Saint Walthen, Abbot of Melrose*, which he dedicated to William, King of Scotland, and *Lives* of Saints Kentigern and Helen have also been attributed to him. His command of Latin rhetoric was much admired by his contemporaries.

Jocelin made a great effort to make his *Life* of Saint Patrick a spiritually uplifting one. The 'Proeme' gives a clear idea of how he viewed his task, and shows why the Normans found it necessary to rewrite Saint Patrick's *Life*. He describes exactly the sort of problems which a person of literary sensibility, but with no knowledge of the literary tastes and habits of Gaelic Ireland, would encounter when reading the *Tripartite Life* in one of its Latin versions, as he undoubtedly did:

> Wherefore in reading the Lives and Acts of the Saints, composed in a rude manner of barbarous dialect, disgust is often excited, and not seldom tardiness of belief. And hence it is, that the life of the most glorious Priest PATRICK, the Patron and Apostle of Ireland, so illustrious in signs and miracles, being frequently written by illiterate persons, through the confusion and obscurity of the style, is by most people neither liked nor understood, but is held in weariness and contempt. Charity therefore urging us, we will endeavour by reducing them to order, to collect what are confused, when collected to compose them into a volume, and when composed, to season them, if not with all the excellence of our language, at least with some of its elegance.

Jocelin's work, which is as long as many a modern biography – 262 pages divided into 196 chapters – is essentially a compilation of all available material, set out in a logical sequence. It is designed to appeal to Ireland's new ruling class, who were representative of mainstream English and continental Roman Catholicism.

He organizes his material into topics, although the chapters are not labelled as such: childhood and youth, the early stages of the Irish mission, its later developments, miracles attributed to the saint in his maturity, acts, sermons, prophecies, and finally the circumstances surrounding his death.

The childhood miracles are amplified versions of the folk-tales told in the *Tripartite*. The idle youth described by the historical Patricius as paying little heed to his priests and teachers is turned into a veritable paragon by Jocelin. Even before his slavery he is outstandingly devout, as befitted the saintly image of Jocelin's day:

> Entering therefore and going forward in the slippery path of youth, he held his feet from falling, and the garment that nature had woven for him, unknowing of a stain, he preserved whole, abiding a Virgin in the flesh and in the spirit . . . he applied his mind to the study of letters, but chiefly to the psalms and hymns and to Spiritual songs, and retaining them in his memory, and continually singing them to the *Lord*.

The earliest part of Jocelin's *Life* follows the facts that Muirchú gleaned from the *Confession*, but they are embellished, this time in line with an orthodox image of sainthood. Jocelin's approach to his material is eclectic: he adds 'miracles' which are in fact part of the folk-tale tradition, some of the prophecies are culled from the bardic tales of Patrick, other bits have been brought in from the Annals, and he also includes stock miracles, stories associated at this period with innumerable other saints.

Jocelin is a conscientious writer, and does his best to enliven the list of Saint Patrick's miracles, many of which involve raising from the dead. His relief is outspoken when he comes to a miracle of a different nature. A certain nun having conceived a terrible lust for Patrick's favourite disciple, the golden-voiced Benignus, feigned illness in order to bring him to her bedside. Saint Patrick knew her intentions, but nevertheless told Benignus to go to her. Benignus entered the nun's house and made the sign of the cross. Jocelin continues:

> Wonderful was the event, and marvellous; unwonted indeed, yet exceedingly profitable. The damsel raising her eyes at his entrance, beheld Benignus very terrible in his stature, and his face as breathing forth flames; and she beheld herself bright with fire both within and without, and Saint PATRICK standing nigh, and covering his head with his hands. And from that hour even unto the end of her life, was the fire of human love extinguished in her bosom, as if her body were of stone or wood, and not of flesh. And afterward she loved Saint Benignus with a pure and saintly love; and she confessed that through his merits Saint PATRICK had snatched her from the fire of Hell.

Jocelin is unable to resist adding a comment: 'Now, for me, I do much more admire this quickening and refreshing of the soul into life, than the raising up of any man from death.'

It is not just the repetitiousness of many of the Patrician miracles which makes Jocelin's literary endeavour a difficult task. He is also the first biographer writing for a non-Irish audience, and is faced with the problem of the vast number of Irish place and proper names which are associated with Saint Patrick. Ever since Giraldus non-Irish speakers have bemoaned the 'uncouthness' of the Irish language. It is, of course, a most beautiful language: the charge arises simply because the rules of pronunciation in Gaelic differ from those in English. As has often been observed, it is a supreme arrogance on the part of English-speakers to assume that there is only one correct set of rules for the pronunciation of the letters of the Roman alphabet, and that the highly inconsistent English one. But in Giraldus's and Jocelin's day even the sound of correctly pronounced Gaelic was considered barbarous: Jocelin lists, for example, the Latinized names of six bishops, and then adds: '... to mention the names of their bishoprics, we for good reason omit: for in many instances we avoid the names of places and persons, that we may not by their uncouth barbarousness occasion disgust or horror to cultivated ears.'

Jocelin is not entirely innocent of a milder form of Giraldus's contempt for the native Irish. One example occurs in the course of a stock miracle: the national apostle, who is famed for his abstinence, conceals a piece of swine's flesh in a vessel 'thinking rightly that he might thus satisfy his appetite privily, which should he openly do, he would become to his brethren a stone of offence, and a stumbling block of reproach.' However, before Patrick starts eating, God sends a servant to remind him that God is all-seeing. Patrick, overwhelmed by remorse, 'abjured the eating of flesh meat, even through the rest of his life.' Patrick asks the angel Victor who has been sent to comfort him, for a sign of God's forgiveness:

Then the Angel bade Patrick to bring forth the hidden meats and put them into Water; and he did as the Angel bade; and the flesh-meats being plunged into the Water and taken thereout, immediately became Fishes. This miracle did Saint PATRICK often relate to his disciples, that they might restrain the desire of their Appetites.

Jocelin then describes a ruse stemming from this miracle by which the Irish allow themselves to eat meat in Lent:

But many of the Irish, wrongfully understanding this miracle, are wont on St Patrick's day, which always falls in the time of Lent, to plunge Flesh-Meats into Water, when plunged in to take out, when taken out to dress, when dressed to eat, and call them Fishes of Saint PATRICK. But hereby every Religious Man will learn to restrain his appetite, and not to eat meat at forbidden seasons, little regarding what ignorant and foolish Men are wont to do.

The custom of eating boiled meat in Lent and referring to it as 'Saint Patrick's fishes' persisted down the centuries: accounts of the practice were recorded by the Folklore Commission as recently as the 1930s. Also, in some parts of the country, goose is known as Saint Patrick's fish. This euphemism enabled even the most devout parish priest to indulge in a portion of goose flesh on a Friday.

Jocelin's *Life* is not without its faults. His efforts to elevate his subject-matter sometimes lead him to ruin a perfectly good folk-story, by stripping it of its more fantastic elements. At other times he tends to exaggerate Patrick's miraculous achievements, often to no discernible purpose.

But his thoroughness provided later writers of abridged *Lives* of Patrick with an abundance of material, presented in elegant, persuasive language. Jocelin's is not the *Life* to choose if burrowing for historical facts. Its charm is quite other: an experience of medieval hagiography of a high literary calibre and also a most intriguing exercise in the un-Irishing of a legend which, up until Jocelin, was the property and creation of the native Christian tradition, inherited from the earliest Irish Christians.

The tradition that Saint Patrick was buried at Down – now Downpatrick – remains strong to this day. Even though all the authorities agree that he is not buried there, the stream of visitors to his 'grave' is so persistent that it is signposted in the town. The 'grave' is situated in the cathedral grounds. In the nineteenth century the faithful used to take a handful of earth from the site home with them and visitors were so numerous that there was serious concern that the hill on which the cathedral stood would be eroded by this superstitious habit. To prevent it, a large granite slab was commissioned from a sculptor in 1900 and placed over the 'grave'. It is engraved with the word 'Patric' and a simple cross, and it is still prayed at by visitors, even though most of them are well aware that the saint is not buried there. When I visited it on 17 March, 1986 it was strewn with daffodils.

The present-day descendant of the Norman John de Courcy who discovered the grave of Brigid, Patrick and Colmcille, believes in the tradition that his ancestor disturbed Saint Patrick's bones, and with good reason. John de Courcy (b.1941), Lord Kingsale and premier baron of Ireland, relates a family tradition which claims that the original John de Courcy was cursed by a local holy man for disturbing the bones of Saint Patrick, and told, in an authentically *Tripartite*-style curse, that his line would live forever and never prosper.

A glance at the de Courcy family history reveals that the de Courcys do indeed display a remarkable ability for losing whatever land, wealth or privileges are bestowed upon them. Ireland's premier baron is, at the time of writing, an unemployed plumber with not a penny to his name. As he lacked the resources to look after what is left of his only remaining ancestral property, the ruins of de Courcy Castle at the Old Head of Kinsale, in 1986 he sold the deeds to the townspeople of Kinsale for a nominal fifty pence.

5

SAINT PATRICK'S PURGATORY: LOUGH DERG

Saint Patrick's Purgatory is situated on Station Island in Lough Derg, Co. Donegal. From the earliest days of the Irish Christian church to the present time it has been a place of pilgrimage. An average of 30,000 pilgrims travel to Lough Derg every year during the pilgrimage season (1 June–15 August) to spend three days fasting and praying, and submit themselves to an all-night vigil on Station Island.

Nowadays Saint Patrick's Purgatory is referred to by those who go there as Lough Derg, and, by the uninitiated, as Station Island, a relatively modern name. It comes from the Latin *statio*, and on Lough Derg is used to refer to a penitential exercise called a 'station'. This is a set pattern of silent prayers undertaken while walking, standing and kneeling at circles of stones known as the penitential beds.

Ireland was famous throughout medieval Europe as the location of Saint Patrick's Purgatory. Sir Shane Leslie, whose family were the landlords of Station Island for many years, did much research into the history of the place. He describes Saint Patrick's Purgatory as:

> . . . the medieval rumour which terrified travellers, awed the greatest criminals, attracted the boldest of knight errantry, puzzled the theologian, englamoured Ireland, haunted Europe, influenced the current view and doctrines of Purgatory, and not least inspired Dante.

Yet Saint Patrick's Purgatory does not feature in any of the early *Lives* of Patrick, not even in Tirechán's detailed list of places visited and churches founded by the first bishop of Armagh. Its name does not occur among the many included in the *Tripartite Life*. Nor is Lough Derg mentioned by Jocelin, but a description was added by another hand to some later editions, for by the thirteenth century no Life of Saint Patrick would be complete for continental audiences without an account of the famous Cave of Purgatory.

Giraldus is not one to let such a good story get away. This is how he tells it:

> There is a lake on the bounds of Ulster containing a double island. The one part has a church of approved religion. It is very lovely and beautiful. It has been made incomparably glorious by the visitation of Angels and the visible throng of local saints. The other part is very rough and horrible and is said to be given over to the demons only. It remains almost continually open to the visible crowding and possession of evil spirits. The other part has nine Pits, in any of which, should someone dare to spend the night (which has been proved and recorded of daring men at times) he is immediately seized by evil spirits and is tortured all night with such heavy pains, and tormented so incessantly with so many grievous and unspeakable torments of fire and water, that with morning there is scarcely any or only the dregs of life surviving in his wretched body. They say that if anyone endures these torments under an injunction of penance, he will not undergo any further pains in the world below unless he has committed fresh sins. The place is called St Patrick's Purgatory by the Natives.

Giraldus has, as usual, got it slightly wrong. There were not nine pits, and neither was the island divided into angelic and demonic halves. The 'Purgatory' was a cave in which, after a preparation of fifteen days' strict fasting and penance, the pilgrim was locked for a twenty-four-hour vigil during which he supposedly suffered the horrors of Purgatory. Many pilgrims, the rumour ran, did not live to tell the tale.

The early history of Lough Derg is vague. It was traditionally visited by Patrick in 445, when he spent some time there alone in prayer and penance. The next traditional belief about Lough

Derg concerns one Saint Dabheoc the elder, who was in charge of its monastic settlement until his death in 516. Nothing more is known of its monastery until about the year 836 when it was destroyed by the Vikings. The historical records of Lough Derg begin in 1135 when the Canons Regular of Saint Augustine took charge of the place. They were sent there from Armagh, probably by Saint Malachy, the Primate of Armagh, in the course of his twelfth-century ecclesiastical reforms, to minister to the pilgrims who frequented the place. None of the authorities nowadays doubt that Lough Derg was a place of pilgrimage long before the arrival of the Canons Regular.

Lough Derg throughout the Middle Ages existed with a twin identity. In England and throughout continental Europe it acquired mythological fame as the location of the most testing, often fatal, trial available to the faithful – a descent into a cave where one could at great peril see and experience Purgatory – while among the Irish it continued to be a retreat for intensive prayer and less spectacular forms of penance.

It must be remembered that at this time Ireland represented the very edge of the known world to the European mind, and was not thought of as an accessible or hospitable destination. No one visited that remote and backward country who had not a very good reason for doing so.

Lough Derg is still a strange and eerie place. It is four miles from the nearest small town, Pettigo, a town which in any other European country would be referred to as a village. The road passes through bogland with no signs of habitation on either side. It ends at the shore of the lake, where, in the pilgrimage season, visitors must wait for an open boat to carry them over the five-minute crossing to Station Island.

Since Norman times many pilgrims have written accounts of their visit to Station Island, and it is remarkable how little the physical aspect of Lough Derg seems to have changed over the centuries. The dark lake, six miles by four, is surrounded by low hills covered with monotonous dark brown and dark green vegetation. Some of its shores are bogland, others are covered in heather, and there is one softwood plantation. Its small islands are overgrown with scrub; some of the larger ones are wooded. Only a few small whitewashed farmhouses overlook it.

Lough Derg is the sort of remote and memorable place that tends to attract legends and, because it is situated in Ireland, there is of course no shortage of them. Long before the arrival of Saint Patrick, it seems more than likely that Lough Derg was associated with druidical practices. Its waters, because of the bogs that surround it, are unusually dark. The many exposed rocks, locally glorified by the name of islands, suggest the shapes of half-submerged monsters. It is easy to understand how the place must have stirred the imagination of the ancients.

The medieval legend of Saint Patrick's Purgatory began with the pilgrimage to Lough Derg of a certain soldier of fortune known as the Knight Owen. His name appears in medieval manuscripts as Owain, Owein, Miles, Ennius, Oengus or Oenus among others. His pilgrimage to Lough Derg is usually dated to 1147 because he says that he followed his penance on the island by going on a crusade to the Holy Land during the reign of King Stephen. Such a crusade took place between 1147 and 1149.

On returning from the crusade the Knight Owen went to England where he met the superior of a Cistercian monastery who had recently been granted lands in Ireland. He was about to send one of his monks, Gilbert, to open a new house of the order there. The monk needed a companion for the potentially hazardous journey, and the Knight Owen was offered the job. In the course of their travels he told Gilbert of his extraordinary experiences at Lough Derg, and Gilbert recounted them to another Cistercian, Henry of Saltrey, who wrote them down.

Owen had a sinful past, and confessed himself to the Bishop of Clogher, in whose diocese Lough Derg is to be found. He pleaded with the bishop for permission to make his penance in Saint Patrick's Purgatory. The bishop, as was the custom, did his utmost to dissuade the knight from such a dangerous undertaking, but eventually gave his permission. Owen spent fifteen days at Lough Derg fasting and doing penance in preparation for his ordeal. The prior warned him that many who had entered the cave known as Saint Patrick's Purgatory had vanished without a trace, but Owen would not be dissuaded.

The prior told Owen that, once inside the cave, he should look for a hall built on pillars where God would provide him with guides for his journey. Owen stumbled through the darkness until he came to such a place, where he was advised by fifteen white-robed men. They told him that when they departed terrible demons would try to persuade him to return to the entrance of the cave. If he succumbed to their threats he would perish. He was to remain strong in his faith and call upon the name of his God.

As soon as the men disappeared, demons in their hordes descended upon Owen and tried to tempt him to return to the mouth of the cave. He remained steadfast, and was led by the demons through the punishments of Hell. He saw sinful souls under torment in diverse manners beloved of the medieval imagination: being prodded with white-hot nails, immersed in boiling metal, suffering extremes of cold, sat upon by hideous toads, nailed to red-hot wheels, and so on. Owen participated in the suffering but whenever he called out God's name he was released from pain.

He was brought to the top of a high mountain where thousands of dread-filled souls shivered in the cold blasts of the north wind. A hurricane blew Owen and the whole shivering throng into a foul and stinking stream where demons drowned all who attempted to float. Owen called on God and managed to struggle out on to the bank. Next the demons showed him the entrance to Hell itself and told him that unless he agreed to return to the cave's entrance he would stay there for ever. When he again defied them, the demons threw him into Hell. He was so terrified that he forgot momentarily to call out God's name, and he descended into a fiery pit which contained many millions of souls. When he remembered to call on God he was instantly cast out of the pit, but found himself in the hands of more devils.

These fiends brought him to another stinking stream filled with tormented souls and showed him a bridge across it called the Bridge of the Three Impossibilities. It was so high, so narrow and so slippery that any human who tried to cross it always fell into the stream below. However, having prayed especially hard in preparation, Owen made it across the bridge.

He travelled a short distance and came to a brightly lit wall. He passed through a jewelled golden gate and was met by a procession of radiant dignitaries who showed him the beauty of their land. He was told that these were souls who had passed through Purgatory, and were awaiting entrance into Heaven. Owen was told that he himself had passed through Purgatory with the demons, and would never have to go there again. All those he had seen so far, except the souls in the pit of Hell, would eventually come to this place on their way to Heaven.

Owen was led to the top of another high mountain, this time one of blissful beauty, where he spent some time in prayer. His greatest desire was to stay this close to Paradise, but he was told that it was his duty to return to the world and tell others of his experience. He was led back to the entrance of the penitential cave. When the Prior came to release Owen after twenty-four hours he found him more dead than alive. He had to be carried from the cave, and there was great rejoicing and thanksgiving for his survival.

Whether the Knight Owen's account of Purgatory is true, and indeed whether the knight existed at all, has been much debated. There is certainly an element of good timing about its appearance. The doctrine of Purgatory was still evolving in the mid-twelfth century, and the trials of the Knight Owen, whether designed with a didactic purpose or not, helped to explain the new doctrine vividly and to ensure that it made an impression on the popular imagination.

Whatever the origin of the story of the cave, it is evident that, in its day, Henry of Saltrey's account of the Knight Owen's adventures became the medieval equivalent of a best-seller. The fame of the Purgatory continued to grow and spread over the next 200 years, until the legend became a part of the general knowledge of the time. One index of its popularity is the fact that 150 manuscript copies of Henry of Saltrey's *Tractatus de Purgatorio S. Patricii* survive today in European libraries and about 300 more give his story in translation. Medieval historians included Owen's story in their chronicles, spreading its fame ever wider.

Adventurers from England, France, Italy, Hungary, Holland, Flanders, Spain and Switzerland travelled across Europe, sometimes alone and on foot, sometimes with large retinues, to the remote lough in the north-west of Ireland in order to inflict the experience of Purgatory on themselves. Early maps of Ireland give vastly disproportionate prominence to the Purgatory. Its earliest mention is on a map of 1413. In the Argentine Ptolemy Map of 1513, according to Shane Leslie, 'it fills as large a corner of Ireland as a county.' Leslie adds 'in Martin Behaim's World Map of 1492 the sole entry for *Urland* is *St Paterici Fegbeur* which is the German version of the name.'

Betelius, who printed a map of Ireland upside down *c.* 1560, shows the Purgatory as a large cave in the south-east (as opposed to the north-west) corner of the country, and gives it the same prominence as the two other places in the country he deemed important: the city of Armagh and Lough Foyle. Incidentally, Betelius makes the following comment on Hibernia, which gives some idea of what, even in the late sixteenth century, a pilgrim to that country was led to expect: '50 Bishoprics – nothing born poisonous – the race uncouth of customs, rejoicing in war, pillage and music.'

Nevertheless, they travelled to this barbarous outpost – Godalh from France in 1248, his countryman the Sire de Beaujeu around 1300, Georgius Crissaphan from Hungary in 1353, Louis de Sur of France and two Italians, Malatesta of Rimini and Nicholas de Baccariis, in 1358. From England came John Bonham in 1360, Sir William de Lisle in 1394 and William Staunton of Durham in 1406. Twenty-two of these pilgrims left written accounts of their experiences in Purgatory, most of which follow the pattern set by the Knight Owen's adventures, with personal variations and elaborations.

An embellishment to the Knight Owen's ordeal was provided by the practice, adopted at Lough Derg during the fourteenth century, of treating the pilgrim, after fifteen days of fasting and penance, to the Office of the Dead followed by a solemn Requiem

Mass on the night before entering the cave. The Mass was celebrated while the pilgrim lay in his coffin. Little wonder, perhaps,
that those who entered the Purgatory succumbed to vivid visionary dreams which had all the appearance of reality.

Cynicism recedes, however, on reading the records left by the
pilgrims. Whatever induced their visions, there is little doubt
that they underwent a deeply felt religious experience. Many of
the pilgrims devoted themselves to a life of fasting, abstinence,
chastity and penance after their visit to Lough Derg. Others were
honest enough to admit that not much at all happened to them in
the dreaded cave. One such account was given to the historian
Froissart by the English knight Sir William de Lisle:

> Then he said: 'When I and my fellow were entered and past
> the gate of the cellar, that was called the Purgatory of Saint Pat-
> rick, and that we were descended and gone down there three
> or four paces, descending down as into a cellar, a certain hot
> vapour rose against us and strake so into our heads that we
> were fain to sit down on the stairs which are of stone. And
> after we had sat there a season, we had great desire to sleep and
> so fell asleep and slept there all night.' Then I demanded if in
> their sleep they knew where they were or what visions they
> had. He answered me that in sleeping they entered into great
> imaginations and marvellous dreams otherwise than they
> were wont to have in their chambers and on their beds. 'In the
> morning we were awakened, they opened the bolt, for so we
> had ordered and we issued out and within a short season clean
> forgot our dreams and visions; wherefore we thought and
> think all that matter was but a phantasy.'

More spectacular were the experiences reported by the Hun-
garian knight Georgius Crissaphan. In the course of his visionary
sojourn in the cave in 1353 he was given secret messages for the
Primate of Ireland; Edward, the King of England and the Queen,
his mother; John, the King of France; the Pope, Innocent VI; and
the Sultan of Babylon, no less. Georgius delivered each message
in person, a task which must have taken him years, but it had to
be done as the messages were entrusted to him by the Blessed
Archangel Michael himself:

And when the Blessed Archangel Michael laid these embassies aforesaid on the part of Our Lord upon Georgius saying: Such and such you will say unto such and such, George said: How will the Kings aforesaid believe that he had been in Purgatory, Hell and Heaven and spoken face to face with an Archangel? The angel gave him most sure and secret signs unknown to mortal except to those to whom Georgius was sent.

In 1397 the Purgatory was visited by a Spanish count, Raymond de Perelhos, who was trying to get in touch with King John of Aragon who had just died. He located the king in Purgatory, but could not find out from him why he had not been sent straight to heaven. De Perelhos also met a kinswoman of whose death he had had no knowledge before leaving home. She explained her presence in Purgatory as being a punishment for having spent so much time 'in trimming and painting her face'.

While there is a certain repetitive similarity in the descriptions of the tortures of Hell and the wonders of Heaven, each pilgrim brings his own individual background into the experience. William Staunton, for example, a native of Durham who made the pilgrimage in 1406, was helped by encountering his very own patron saints, John of Bridlington and Saint Ives, who acted as his guides as he began his descent into Purgatory.

There is a marked divergence between the continental experience of Lough Derg and the native Irish experience of the place. It had been a place of pilgrimage for Irish penitents long before the arrival of the Normans, and continued to be one after the arrival of the Canons Regular of Saint Augustine.

We have one remarkable story which, if there is any truth in it, indicates the important place that the Lough Derg pilgrimage held for Irish chieftains. According to the seventeenth-century historian Geoffrey Keating, Tiernan O'Rourke, Prince of Breffni, made a pilgrimage to Lough Derg in 1152. His wife, Devorgilla, took advantage of his absence to arrange an elopement with Diarmuid MacMurrough of Leinster. O'Rourke waged war on MacMurrough in order to reclaim his wife, and MacMurrough's defeat led him to offer his services to Henry II in return for

Henry's help in regaining his lands, thus precipitating the Norman invasion.

Neither O'Rourke (if he really did make the pilgrimage) nor any of the other Irish pilgrims left written accounts of terrifying experiences in Patrick's Purgatory. The Irish did not go to Lough Derg in search of spiritual adventure: they went to do penance in the manner established by the ascetic monks of the early Celtic church. Repetition of prayers combined with physical hardship was their idea of penance.

For evidence of the native experience of Lough Derg we are fortunate to have the testimony of the many poets who made the pilgrimage over the centuries. The mood of the Irish writers on Lough Derg is far removed from the colourful, event-filled dreams reported by the Europeans. The Irish poets produced heart-rending verse filled with petitions for mercy to Christ, Saint Patrick and their favourite saints, and laments for their own sinfulness. Often they chastised themselves for the difficulty they found in reaching a suitably emotional state of penitence, as does the thirteenth-century bard, Donnchadh Mór O Dálaigh in the following poem. This was, to judge by the number of extant manuscripts in which it occurs, a great favourite among Irish pilgrims to Lough Derg:

Alas for my visit to Lough Derg to weep thy wounds and stripes, O Lord of its cells and bells, seeing I can press no tear from my eye. Alas, O Lord, what shall I do with my eye which, after doing all the evil it could, is not moist, and with my heart that seeks not peace? Lamenting my sins, but without heart-sore or sorrow or grief – not so did Patrick, chief of clergy, seek God ! . . .

Buried alive in this Cave, this strait hard prison of stone, I can find, alas! no tears after all my deeds of sin and pride. O sinful body, as thou art set on going to Hell, what thou suffrest now, naked and fasting, is too little for thee. We all, clergy and laity, shall scream aloud on Monday, but the tear, which was not shed in proper time, shall not then avail. O withered body, for which Christ was crucified, take now thy choice – tears of penance and God's possession or sojourn in the House of Pain.

O Son of Mary, Creator of all, who shunned not the death of the three nails, I am ashamed for this pilgrimage to Lough Derg with my heart as hard as stone.

Within the native Irish tradition there is no mention of struggles with demons of the other world. Each and every one of the poets is concerned with repentance. Nothing could contrast more strongly with the way that Lough Derg was treated in the continental tradition. Probably the most influential early work was a rhyming lay translated from Latin into French by the troubadour poet Marie de France, *c.* 1190. Other verse renderings of the Knight Owen's adventures survive in manuscript in early Middle English, none of any great literary interest.

It has been argued that the tale of the Knight Owen had a direct influence on Dante's *Divine Comedy*, and it is indeed most likely that Dante was familiar with the tale, such was its popularity in his lifetime. A close reading of Dante can reveal many parallels with the visions reported by pilgrims to the Purgatory, but this is not conclusive evidence for direct influence. There were many such tales of visionary journeys through the underworld in circulation in the Middle Ages. The best known before Dante is the sixth book of Virgil's *Aeneid*. The tale of Saint Patrick's Purgatory occupies a minor place in visionary literature.

Not all commentators are convinced of the historical reality of the Knight Owen. Shane Leslie who, for all his assiduousness in collecting and publishing material related to Lough Derg, had some very odd ideas at times, insists that the Knight Owen was a mythical figure, one of the knights of the Round Table. If that was the case, then either the monk Henry of Saltrey was a liar and a forger or he never existed at all, but was invented as a sophisticated framing device by some Norman romancer. Whether Owen's tale was historical or not (and I strongly suspect that it was not), it provided the *primum mobile* for Lough Derg's medieval fame.

That fame was, in the end, its undoing. Pilgrims, it appears, were looked on as a useful source of income by both the prior and the local bishop. This was revealed by a pious mendicant monk from Eymstadt in Holland. He had received permission from his

Order to travel to renowned places of pilgrimage, dependent only on the alms given to him by people he met along the way. On his arrival at Lough Derg, the monk was told by the prior that he could not enter the cave without permission from both the Bishop of Clogher, in whose diocese the Purgatory lay, and the local chieftain. The monk approached the Bishop of Clogher first, but because of his obvious poverty he was denied access to the bishop by the servants. When the monk finally gained an audience with the bishop he was told that he would have to pay for the permit. The monk pointed out that he was penniless and, even if he had the money, to charge pilgrims for such permits was simony and he would not pay. After a long delay and much difficulty he was given the necessary document. He had then to go through exactly the same procedure with the local chieftain, whom he refers to as 'the Prince of that territory'. The Monk of Eymstadt finally got back to Lough Derg only to discover that the prior was also demanding a sum of money from him.

The persistent monk somehow talked his way past the prior and was at last admitted to the famous cave, where he saw not a single vision, but merely suffered cold and discomfort. Not surprisingly, he lodged a complaint with Pope Alexander VI. After a papal investigation the mendicant monk had the enormous satisfaction of returning to Ireland bearing a papal order for the closure of the cave.

However, the pilgrimage was not easily suppressed. In 1503, only six years after its closure, it was re-opened by order of Pope Pius III at the request of the Archbishop of Armagh. This time, however, it became an Irish pilgrimage, and the stream of adventuring foreigners ceased.

Because of its remoteness and its mainly Gaelic clientele, the pilgrimage survived the Reformation and the dissolution of the monasteries by Henry VIII. Records exist of the way in which the pilgrimage was being performed around the year 1600, and they bear a remarkable similarity to its form today. The pilgrimage lasted nine days then; nowadays it lasts for three. The fast was broken once a day by bread and water; nowadays it is broken once a day by bread and black tea or coffee. No food whatever was taken on the day before or after the vigil, and on emerging from the cave the seventeenth-century pilgrim plunged three times under lake water as a symbol of purification, an ordeal which modern pilgrims are spared. The total number of Aves, Paters and Creeds recited silently during each 'Station' – 280 – is almost the same today as it was in 1600. Then, as now, pilgrims were expected to make a total of nine stations.

There was far more veneration of relics involved in the 1600 station, for the simple reason that in the centuries intervening between 1600 and today the buildings of Lough Derg were several times reduced to rubble, and all 'superstitious relics' thrown into the lake.

The history of the pilgrimage from the Reformation to the early nineteenth century reflects the turbulence of Irish life during that period. The two events which most affected the remote area of Lough Derg were the Plantation of Ulster and the proscription of Catholicism by the Penal Laws.

The land around Lough Derg, including Station Island, was traditionally an ancient sanctuary area and therefore church property, or termon land. Under Irish law it was held in trust for the church by the Magrath family. In order to retain the right to use this land, the Magraths surrendered it to the Crown, and it was re-granted to them in 1610 for a rent of ten pounds a year. In June of 1632, following the Reformation and the establishment of the (Protestant) Church of Ireland, the pilgrimage was suppressed by order of the Privy Council of Ireland. James Magrath, who was making a fair income – estimated at over £200 a year – from his ownership of ferry rights to the island, did not carry out the order of destruction, and was arrested. A new order was made out, and among those held responsible for carrying out the destruction of the buildings on the island was the Protestant Bishop of Clogher, James Spottiswoode. He was exceptionally thorough in his destruction of the buildings and relics on the island, leaving nothing but stones and rubble behind him, and for the next few years his vigilance ensured that no pilgrims crossed to the island. The pilgrimage, however, did not die out: pilgrims assembled on the lake shore, and performed their rituals there.

Not even a personal letter from Queen Henrietta Maria, con-

The prominence given to Saint Patrick's Purgatory on Lough Derg in Betelius' map of Ireland in 1590 is indicative of the importance that the shrine had on the continent at that time. The map is inverted, with the Purgatory appearing in the south-east corner instead of the north-west. The comment in the box at the top of the map gives some idea of what visitors to Hibernia were led to expect in those days. It concludes: '50 Bishoprics – nothing born poisonous – the race uncouth of customs, rejoicing in war, pillage and music'.

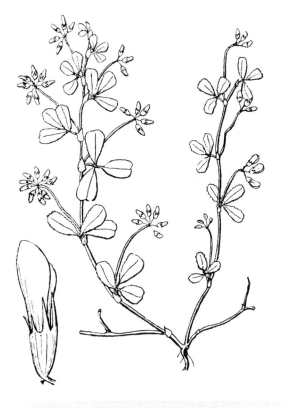

The shamrock is not a unique genus of plant: after many years of argument botanists now agree that the 'shamrock' which the Irish pick in mid-March is in fact the winter resting stage of the white or yellow clover.

Trifolium repens.

Above: Although the shamrock is unofficially recognized throughout the world as a symbol of Irishness, the closest it has come to recognition by the Irish government is as a logo for the national airline, Aer Lingus. The officially recognized symbol of Ireland is the harp which appears on all Irish coins.

Below: The only relic among the treasures associated with Saint Patrick in Dublin's National Museum that actually dates from the fifth century is this iron bell (*right*). Even if it is not, as is traditionally believed, the bell used by the saint, he probably carried one very like it. The beautiful artifact on the left was made to enshrine the Bell in the late eleventh century. The interlacements on the front are of gold, those on the sides of silver.

Saint Patrick's Day fills a convenient gap between Saint Valentine's Day and Easter, hence the booming trade in 'green greetings cards' which can be divided neatly into the vulgar and the sentimental. The vulgar strain often emphasizes drunkenness, a tradition with origins in rural eighteenth century Ireland, while the sentimentalism can be traced back to the mass emigrations of the nineteenth century.

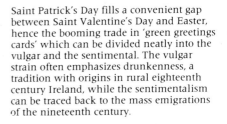

beannachtaí na féile pádraig

PATRICK'S DAY!

S.PATRICIVS HIBERNIÆ APOSTOLVS
Claruit Anno Domini CCCCLVIII.

T. Messingham fecit

Above and left: The familiar image of Saint Patrick as a bearded patriarch in bishop's robes with mitre and crozier, crushing the saints under his feet, can be traced back to the engraving by Thomas Messingham which appeared in 1624. Although wildly anachronistic it served a useful purpose for the Catholic church in that it established visually Patrick's status as the father of Irish Christianity and his episcopal links with Rome. Within Catholic circles it remains the preferred image of Saint Patrick.

Right: Loegaire accompanied by Druids and warriors watches Patrick kindle the Paschal fire on the Hill of Tara.

Lives of Saint Patrick were enormously popular in the latter half of the nineteenth century, particularly if they contained romantic engravings which allowed themselves the same historical licence as the *Lives*.

Left: Ornate Celtic-style borders were a feature of some nineteenth-century *Lives*. Note the shamrocks on the border.

Above left: Most of the few pre-Reformation representations of Saint Patrick to survive in Ireland are on stone crosses. Many of these are too badly weathered to ascertain details, but on this limestone slab from Faughart churchyard, Co. Louth, it is possible to see a youngish, beardless saint.

Above right: Since the emergence of knowledge of the historical Saint Patrick in the late nineteenth century, the Protestant church has preferred to picture him as a beardless young Romano-Briton, as is seen in this stained-glass window in St Mary's Church, Thame, *c.* 1926.

Left: The work of the Harry Clarke Studios is characterized by its use of dense, jewel-like colour and pre-Raphaelite oramentation. Commissioned for the Catholic church at Balbriggan, Co. Dublin, in 1922, their representation of Saint Patrick lighting the Paschal fire at Tara is a restrained and dignified version of the familiar bearded patriarch.

The tradition of parading in the streets to the music of Irish bands on Saint Patrick's Day has its origins in New York and Boston in the late eighteenth century, when such parades were sometimes used by the military for recruiting purposes. Dublin's American-style parade was originally organized mainly for the benefit of tourists, and attracts about a quarter of a million spectators. It is dwarfed by Manhattan's parade which takes over Fifth Avenue for some six hours, and is the inspiration for other parades worldwide, like the relatively new event in Sydney.

sort of Charles I, written in 1638 to the Irish Viceroy, Lord Wentworth, could persuade the authorities to allow the pilgrimage to reopen. Nor were the efforts of the papal nuncio Rinuccini any more successful in restoring the pilgrimage.

James Magrath, seeing no likelihood of any future income from ferry rights on his land around Lough Derg, made over the lease to James Spottiswoode, with the ironic result that the famous site of Catholic pilgrimage was, temporarily at least, in the hands of the Protestant church. The lands passed from Spottiswoode to the Leslie family of Glaslough, whose descendant, Sir Shane, was an avid collector of Lough Derg lore. It was Sir Shane's father, Sir John Leslie, who finally re-invested ownership of the old termon lands in the Catholic church after prolonged litigation earlier this century.

It is a remarkable characteristic of the Lough Derg pilgrimage that official efforts to suppress it have always been thwarted by the persistence of the people, who insist on making it. By the mid-seventeenth century pilgrims were once again praying amid the crudely reconstructed ruins of Station Island. In 1680 the 'buildings' were again destroyed, this time by religious zealots, but by 1704 pilgrims were once again resorting to Station Island in such great numbers that an Act of Queen Anne's government was passed to restrain them. This Act prohibited assembly at Lough Derg under penalty of a ten-shilling fine or, in default of payment, a public whipping. That measure proved as ineffectual as all the others in stopping the pilgrims, and Lough Derg continued to offer a special haven to penitents throughout the eighteenth and nineteenth centuries, as it does to this day.

I was a reluctant pilgrim to Lough Derg. I was, quite simply, terrified of the place – not because of its medieval fame, but because of what it might have to offer in the way of twentieth-century religion. I am a Catholic, but my practice of the religion is erratic and my beliefs are idiosyncratic, probably to the point of heresy.

I tried to get permission from the prior, Monsignor Gerard McSorley, to visit Station Island in pilgrimage season as an observer, and talk to him about the pilgrimage. His reply was polite but firm: 'There will be no problem in speaking to you, but it will not be possible to visit Station Island except as a pilgrim. Only pilgrims are allowed during the season from 1 June to 15 August. Whether or not you wish to come as a pilgrim would be your decision, but to catch the atmosphere of what the pilgrimage is about and even to fully understand Saint Patrick's kind of spirituality it would be almost necessary to go through the experience of the pilgrimage.'

I had done some homework, and knew that while on Station Island I would be expected to stay up praying for the whole of the first night; I would be allowed only one meal a day consisting of black tea and oatcakes or dry bread; and that I would be required to say 1520 Our Fathers, Hail Marys and Creeds while making the stations, plus the prayers involved in hearing Mass four times, Night Prayer and Benediction twice, the one communal Rosary, the Way of the Cross, the Renewal of Baptismal Promises and the Sacrament of Reconciliation.

I arrived at Donegal town by 1 o'clock on Monday, and rebelliously ate the biggest lunch I could find. I should have been fasting since midnight, but I was not intending to go through with the pilgrimage. My plan was to stick it out for as long as I could, gather as much atmosphere and information as possible, then, somehow, get off the island and away from the pious freaks that I expected to meet there.

Pilgrims are asked to arrive between 11 a.m. and 3 p.m. I misjudged the distance from Donegal town to Pettigo, and missed the three o'clock boat by about ten minutes. So did two other women. I parked my car in the lakeside car park and went to the small grey house at the edge of the lake where I was asked for £10 and given in return a leaflet explaining the pilgrimage exercises. An ominous notice beside the pier warned that pilgrims were expected to participate in *all* the exercises of the pilgrimage, and I wondered briefly what happened to those who refused.

I sat in the car reading the previous day's Sunday papers while I waited for a boat. I did not think it would be appropriate to take them, or any other secular literature, along with me on the pilgrimage. A friend who had been to Station Island in the late

1950s had warned me that I would not be allowed to smoke, but I took a supply of cigarettes, just in case. After about ten minutes a child came and told me that a boat was leaving. It was a large open motor-boat, ferrying just myself, two other women, and a young priest carrying two large bottles of Coca-Cola, across to the island. There was no one to meet us on arrival, so I followed the two women, who seemed to know what they were doing, past groups of barefoot pilgrims to the women's hostel.

The first thing you notice on Station Island is the strange quality of the quietness. Even though it is crowded with people, they are all, except the officiating clergy, barefoot. You hear no footsteps or shuffling. Everyone talks in muted voices. The island is so small that you can hear the lake lapping all around it. The lake isolates you from traffic and other everyday background noises. Cameras, radios and cassette recorders are strictly forbidden.

I was assigned to a bunk bed in a large dormitory (alarmingly reminiscent of boarding school) by a young nun, and told that I could leave whatever I did not need on the bed. From the third-floor window there was a beautiful view across the lake to the softwood plantation on the opposite shore: it would cost a fortune to have a hotel room in such a location. I left my socks and shoes under the bed, and went to have a look around the island.

It took about three minutes to see everything. It is tiny. The hostels for men and women face each other across the penitential beds, circles of stones set into a series of hillocks at the lake's edge. Some pilgrims were queueing up to take their turn 'on the beds' while others progressed slowly in and around the stones, praying silently.

The basilica is an architectural triumph on exactly the right scale – a spacious, well-lit octagonal building with a deliberately unadorned interior, save for a spectacular set of stained-glass windows by Harry Clarke depicting the Stations of the Cross and the twelve apostles. Barefoot pilgrims were walking along the circular path outside it with rosaries in hand, praying silently. Others were sitting on benches on the pier, staring out across the lake, or reading. It is possibly the most peaceful place in the world. After only ten minutes on the island I knew there was only one thing to do: participate fully in the pilgrimage and take it seriously.

The most pleasant part of the station is the first part when, having renounced (in silent prayer) the world, the flesh and the devil three times, you walk four times around the basilica saying seven decades of the rosary. After this, at busy times, there is a queue for the beds. You stand in lines five abreast to wait your turn. I noticed with relief that the people in front of me were smoking. Except when in church or on the beds, nearly everyone smokes all the time on Station Island. Several people that I met claimed that they had originally acquired the habit at Lough Derg; others had given up but resumed it for the duration of the pilgrimage. Smoking, it was universally agreed, was a great way to keep yourself awake and to lessen the hunger pangs.

It started to rain while I was queueing for the beds, and there was a light drizzle falling as I made my first station. It demands total concentration. Underfoot there is a mixture of gravel, large slippery stones and small sharp ones. You keep pace with the four people you stood with in the queue, and I soon lost track of which saint's bed I was praying at, and only knew I was in the right place if Father Benignus, with whom I had been chatting in the queue, was there. The repetition of silent prayers quickly becomes monotonous, and even meaningless, as does the repetition of standing, kneeling and walking around each bed, all the while concentrating on what is underfoot and taking care not to trip or stumble. It's a great relief to reach the stage when you can stand in the water's edge (the third last exercise), knowing the station is nearly over, and watch the raindrops fall between the sparse reeds into the rippling black water.

The whole business took well over an hour, and it was difficult to see the point of it. We were supposed to go through it all twice more before Night Prayer and Benediction at 9.30. It was not a pleasant prospect. My knees were already bruised and aching. I retired to the hostel in the hope of getting dry and warm.

The cloakroom of the hostel is a grey-painted room with a large table in the middle and benches around the sides, like an old-fashioned railway station waiting-room. There was a turf fire in one corner. The women seated around it made room for me immediately and offered me a cup of Lough Derg soup – hot water from an urn above the fire sprinkled with salt and pepper. 'Is this your first time?' everyone asks, as an opener for conversation. Some women were knitting, others were reading lurid best-sellers, the younger ones were swapping teenage magazines.'WIVES IN V.D. SHOCK HORROR' ran the headline of yesterday's Sunday paper that a woman opposite me was reading. Old hands are generous with practical tips for first-timers, and a camaraderie quickly develops among those who are to end the night vigil together.

The clergy's attitude, under the enlightened regime of Monsignor McSorley, is one of minimal interference. There is no sense of vigilance, nor of coercion: whether or not you complete the three stations required of you on the first afternoon is an entirely personal matter. Nobody checks up on you. Had I decided to leave early, my decision would have been respected without question. 'This is the people's pilgrimage,' said Monsignor McSorley, when we finally had our chat. 'We're here because people want to come. I made some changes to the liturgy inside the basilica when I took over to bring it up to date, but we made no changes to the outdoor stations. A lot of people can't articulate why they come here. Maybe its atavistic. I think it's a Celtic thing. The beds are a very Celtic sort of practice, it must be somehow imprinted in the imagination. That's what the people want, and it's their pilgrimage. Some people say jokingly that they'd like a drop of milk for their tea, but when it comes down to it they don't really want that sort of change. It would take something away from the experience.'

Free access to the cloakroom of the hostel during the day and the turf fire in its corner are among Monsignor McSorley's innovations, as is the tolerance of smoking, the choice of black coffee instead of tea and the introduction of dry toast to the Lough Derg menu. Following a tip from a seasoned pilgrim, I waited until the last possible moment for my Lough Derg meal. We sat at long refectory tables and plate after plate of toasted cut loaf was served, still hot from the kitchen, while cups were refilled with black tea or coffee as often as one liked. Few people ate the famous traditional oat cakes, which were undercooked and pasty. 'That's taking penance a bit too far,' said the woman sitting next to me.

The all-night vigil is the worst ordeal that Lough Derg has to offer. Once that is over it's all downhill. The hostel is locked after Night Prayer and Benediction, which start at 9.30 p.m., and is not opened until 6.30 the following morning. It is a long vigil: most people have been up since early morning of the day they set out for Station Island, and will not get a chance to sleep until about ten o'clock on the following night – a period of about 38 hours.

We were warned in the sermon at the start of the vigil not to 'lie down and stretch out': if we did so, either during the night or the following day, we would be asked to sit up. We were encouraged to help each other to keep awake. Some groups, I was told, contain officious people who appoint themselves to pester those who doze off. Luckily there were none in my group, and the sight of a dozing figure was more likely to elicit sympathy than criticism.

The night stations are made inside the basilica with one of the pilgrims leading the prayers from the pulpit. Pilgrims walk, stand and kneel, as they did on the beds, wandering around the basilica at whim, which helps to keep one awake. After each station, there is a break of about half an hour.

It was a foul night. It was too cold, wet and windy to follow the Prior's sensible advice and walk around the outside of the basilica in the half-hour breaks between stations. Instead we huddled in the night shelter, a large shed equipped with bare wooden benches. Most people were too tired to read, but the knitters kept knitting, and the smokers kept smoking. Sympathetic remarks were exchanged with whoever happened to sit next to you. The lowest point of the night came while waiting for the sixth station to start at 3.30 a.m., knowing that there was a seventh station to endure at 5 a.m., then Mass, and no prospect of breakfast to reward your efforts.

It was an exceptionally black night. One door of the basilica is left open on the darkness. I have never longed so much to see the light of dawn, and never has it seemed so slow in coming. At last, towards 4.30, the blackness started to fade. At this point the birds on the lake were making more noise than the pilgrims. The silence in the night shelter was broken only by subdued voices. There was no effort at sustained conversation, just isolated remarks: 'Bitter cold'; 'Never again'.

Only ten or fifteen people out of the 360 with whom I made the vigil succumbed to the temptation to doze in the shadows at the back of the church. It was very difficult not to. I managed to fall asleep on my feet, and woke with a start as my knees gave way. But the daylight helped a great deal, and it was a tremendous relief to see the second-day pilgrims joining us for the 6.30 Mass looking fresh and rested after their sleep. It reminds you that by this time tomorrow, you too will have slept, and the pilgrimage will be nearly over.

I expected to meet jaded priests, batty old women and spotty youths with a vocation on Station Island. Instead I met a normal and exceptionally pleasant cross-section of Irish people from all walks of life. It is impossible to put on airs and graces when everyone is walking around barefoot, hungry and badly deprived of sleep. Old and young, male and female, lay and clergy, professionals and workers all mingle together totally at ease. No one affects pious superiority: there is no place for it. It is an atmosphere to which even the most hardened sophisticate must succumb – as Sean O'Faolain demonstrates in his acutely observed story about Lough Derg, *The Lovers of the Lake*.

Many people commented on how nice it was to see so many of the younger generation – the 16–25 age group – on pilgrimage. I found the people with whom I spent the vigil remarkably uncritical of each other, and I heard very few complaints. There was a rumour of bats in the top floor of the women's hostel (a new one is under construction). 'I don't care if there's bats,' said one woman. 'Nothing is going to keep me awake tonight.' And we all agreed.

Reasons for coming on the pilgrimage are as varied as the backgrounds of the pilgrims, but Father Flynn, one of the resident clergy, was able to draw up certain categories: 'Many people come to pray for something specific as a form of petition, perhaps their own health or that of someone in their family. A lot of the young people are here to pray for success in exams. Some people are mourning someone who has died tragically. And many come specifically for the Sacrament of Reconciliation (Confession), people who have perhaps been away from practice for some time, or who have something big on their minds. Lough Derg has a name as a place to come and deal with that sort of thing. We also have folk who come regularly every year as a sort of family tradition. And I suppose some people come from curiosity.' Had he not been such a good representative of the new generation of enlightened Irish clergy, he would have looked at me with hostility when making that last point. Instead he laughed the most frank and open laughter that I have ever heard. Still slightly high after my all-night vigil, I laughed with him, then we both stared in silence across the dark lake.

Whatever the reasons, Lough Derg continues to be a popular place of pilgrimage. Their biggest crowds this century – around 34,000 in a season – occurred in the 1950s. These days a steady 22,000–25,000 pilgrims a year go to Station Island. Several people told me that one reason they come back to Lough Derg is the lack of commercialization in comparison with places like Knock, Fatima, and especially Lourdes. There is one small shop on Station Island, selling religious souvenirs and literature, and cigarettes, all at normal prices. Apart from the very reasonable £10 fee, no other financial demand is made of the pilgrim. The strictly enforced 'no visitors' policy preserves the very special atmosphere of the place. People also like the sense of achievement which accompanies you for a long time after leaving the island – if you can do Lough Derg, you can do anything. It revives and enhances your appreciation of the normal small pleasures of everyday life to an extraordinary extent.

My friend Father Benignus was among the few who turn up in almost every batch of pilgrims who dislike the mechanical nature of the stations, and find the pilgrimage ineffectual. Reacting, perhaps, to the expression on my face, he confided as we completed our first station on the beds that it had done nothing for him. I was inclined to agree: I could not, then, see the point of it. As the night wore on I stopped asking what the point was: it was just something I was doing. Once you have started the pilgrimage it must be completed, whether it seems to give you a spiritual experience or not. There is little sense of anything spiritual happening at the time. It is not until you leave the island that you start to feel the difference, which can be described as a great sense of peace and regeneration, a new perception of yourself in relation to the material world and your own life.

6

THE GREENING OF
SAINT PATRICK

The Irish people, in the late eighteenth century, chose the colour green, the shamrock and Saint Patrick to symbolize their separate identity as a nation. Of these, when independence was finally won in 1922, only the colour green was adopted as part of the new state's official iconography. Yet the shamrock and Saint Patrick have remained potent symbols of Ireland for Irish people and their descendants world-wide, in spite of this lack of official recognition. The greening of Saint Patrick – that is, the place of the shamrock and the colour green in his legend, and the association of both with Irish national identity – is therefore unofficial history. It is the story of what happened to the Saint Patrick legend in the hands of the Irish people, as opposed to its manipulation by the church hierarchy and the ruling classes.

The latter process, as we have seen, began with the work of Muirchú and Tirechán, who used Saint Patrick's traditional associations with Armagh to further the interests of that see. The fact that Armagh, otherwise an insignificant provincial town, today has two magnificent cathedrals and is the seat of the Catholic Primate of all Ireland (although located in a largely Protestant area of British-ruled Northern Ireland) is a heritage of the endeavours of those seventh-century hagiographers.

It was not until the uprisings of the late eighteenth century that Ireland acquired a national identity in the modern sense, that is, an identity based on the claims of a nation aspiring to self-determination, rather than on the claims of one group (Gaelic-speaking and Catholic) within that nation. In the five centuries following the Norman invasion, political and social upheaval had given the intellectual life of the country – both Gaelic and Anglicized – little chance to develop. Ireland, as has often been pointed out, was the only European country to be largely unaffected by the intellectual excitement of the Renaissance.

Yet during all the political turmoil the legend of Saint Patrick continued to develop in the oral tradition. It is during these years, between the Norman invasion in the twelfth century and the Wexford Rebellion of 1798, that the modern, popular image of Saint Patrick emerges. During this period he became associated with the shamrock, with a new, secular celebration of 17 March, with the colour green, and eventually with the emergence of modern nationalism.

The Norman invasion was followed by warfare both among the native Irish and against the Norman settlers. The old Irish way of life was fighting to maintain supremacy over the new English customs. By 1366, when the Statutes of Kilkenny were promulgated, Irish ways seemed to be gaining ground over English, as the newcomers became assimilated into the native way of life. The English crown, which had troubles of its own in France, could not tolerate an independent state to its west and successive monarchs tried, by fair means or foul, to bring their Irish territory under control, with little success. In 1536, Henry VIII announced the establishment of the Church of Ireland, which, like the Church of England, was to be independent of Rome and recognize the English monarch as its head. In 1539 he ordered the dissolution of the monasteries within the Pale. But it was not until the reign of Elizabeth I that the Irish territories began to be effectively brought under the control of the crown.

Elizabeth's system was to replace native landowners with English ones. During the 1580s the Desmond lands in Munster, in the south-west of Ireland, were divided up and given to English settlers (among them Spenser and Raleigh), a move which led to the Nine Years War. The Plantation of Munster, as it was called, was short-lived but set the pattern for the future.

The Plantation of Ulster, in the reign of James I, was a far greater success. The landholders of Ulster, Hugh O'Neill and his allies, left Ireland in 1607 following the defeat of the combined Spanish and Irish forces at the Battle of Kinsale (1601), the so-called 'Flight of the Earls'. Their lands were granted to English and Scottish men of substance on condition that they imported tenants to work the land and establish towns. Over 40,000 settlers moved to the province between 1610 and 1630. The process, once started, was to continue apace. In 1641 Catholic landowners held 59 per cent of the land. This figure fell to about 10 per cent by the year 1700: in other words, by the early 1700s nine-tenths of the land of Ireland was owned by non-Catholics of English and Scottish origin.

Such drastic transference of land ownership was not achieved without much suffering and bloodshed. The Catholic-Gaelic land rebellion of 1641 led to a Catholic Confederacy, a short-lived bid for Catholic supremacy, based at Kilkenny. Cromwell showed no quarter to Catholic Confederates (who also happened to be royalists), massacring a garrison of some 2600 men plus the townspeople at Drogheda shortly after his arrival in 1649.

Even the restoration of the monarchy and the eventual accession of a Catholic Stuart, James II, brought no relief to Ireland. His attempt to restore a Catholic autocracy ended in his overthrow at the Battle of the Boyne (1690) by the forces of the Protestant William of Orange.

The century of relative peace between the Battle of the Boyne and the Wexford Rebellion (1798) was the time of the Penal Laws, when Catholics were barred from any active part in public life, denied the right to own property of any consequence and the right to education, and, for a time at least, forbidden to practise their religion. These were the years when the Ascendancy, the Anglo-Irish Protestants conforming to the established Church of Ireland, flourished, and the remnants of Gaelic Ireland made their final effort to resist total Anglicization.

Many of the most able Irish men preferred to leave their native land and fight in the Catholic armies of Europe, participating in both the victory at Fontenoy and the defeat of the Stuart cause at Culloden. Others enlisted in (or were press-ganged into) the British army and navy. Many of those who joined the British armed services found themselves stationed in America at the outbreak of the War of Independence. Others, mainly Nonconformists from Ulster, made their way to the New World from Ireland independently, in the vanguard of a movement which in the nineteenth century would turn into mass emigration. Those who stayed at home in the latter part of the eighteenth century started to organize against the prevailing oligarchy of the Ascendancy until the example of the French Revolution and the excitement of its notions of liberty and independence led to the uprising of 1798.

It is not a simple matter to trace the connections between the course of history and the changing symbolic use of the figure of Saint Patrick. The oral tradition is, of course, largely undocumented at this stage. It is only chance allusions in written sources that have given historians anything to go on.

The shamrock became connected with Saint Patrick through the tradition that he used this three-leaved plant to explain the Holy Trinity. Although there is no doubt that the tradition had existed for many years, the first written reference to the tale is found in 1727, in a treatise on native Irish plants by the botanist Caleb Threlkeld. He refers to the 'current tradition that by this three-leaved grass, he [Saint Patrick] emblematically set forth to them [the Irish] the mystery of the Holy Trinity.'

The shamrock seems to have acquired its use as an emblem of Ireland at about the same time that it became associated with Saint Patrick – in the late seventeenth and early eighteenth century. The official symbol of Ireland is the harp: surmounted by a crown, it appears in the old arms of Ireland on a blue ground. The nationalist flag displays the same harp, but without a crown above it, on a green ground, and it is featured on twentieth-century Irish coins. The closest that the shamrock gets to official recognition is its use as a logo for the national airline and the Tourist Board. Yet it remains for millions of people world-wide the emblem of Ireland.

The shamrock was originally adopted by the people of Ireland as their national symbol, and it is the people's allegiance to this symbol both at home and abroad, that has ensured its continued use and popularity as an emblem, in spite of a marked lack of recognition by successive governments of the independent state of Ireland. In 1928 the Finance Committee – which included the poet W. B. Yeats – refused to sanction the shamrock as a design for the new coinage on the dubious grounds that the shamrock legend was a new one with only 125 years of history behind it.

The word shamrock is derived from the Irish *seamrog*, a diminutive form of *seamar* – trefoil or clover. The Irish origin of the word is of course highly significant. Its vagueness – literally, 'little three-leaved plant' – has given rise to much discussion among botanists as to exactly which small clover *is* the shamrock. Even today heated arguments can arise among those Irish who pick their own shamrock to wear on 17 March as to whether the correct miniature trefoil is being displayed.

Early Irish art in the style known as *La Tène* (of which the Tara brooch is probably the best known example) is distinguished by its use of abstract forms of decoration. There are no trefoils to be found in pre-Christian Irish art, nor on those artefacts commissioned by the early Christian monks in *La Tène* style. None of the early reliquaries associated with Saint Patrick and now in the collection of the National Museum in Dublin – the Shrine of Saint Patrick's Bell, the Shrine of Saint Patrick's Tooth, and Saint Patrick's Bell itself – is adorned with trefoils.

Trefoils can be found in early Irish illuminated manuscripts, but they do not seem to have any special significance: they are merely one among many decorative elements. As one historian with a remarkable gift for the inappropriate metaphor – known as an Irish bull – has put it, 'the vine and the trefoil are the roots of all Irish leaf ornament.'

In a similar way, and presumably because the three-leaved shape is pleasing to the eye, trefoils can be found on decorative tiles and stonework between the twelfth and sixteenth centuries. There are, for example, two stone lintels from a sixteenth-century town house preserved in Kinsale Museum, one adorned with a shamrock, bearing the date 1574, and the other with a rose encircled by shamrocks. No particular significance should be read into such decorations or into the occasional appearance of trefoils on medieval manuscripts such as the twelfth- or thirteenth-century copy of Giraldus Cambrensis's *History and Topography of Ireland*, known as MS 700 of the National Library of Ireland.

Until recently the only major investigation into the history of the shamrock was a paper published by Nathaniel Colgan in the *Journal of the Royal Society of Antiquaries of Ireland* in 1896 entitled 'The Shamrock in Literature: A Critical Chronology'. All subsequent writers on the topic, myself included, are heavily indebted to this pioneering piece of erudition which its author modestly calls 'a mass of shamrockiana'.

Colgan's findings will be updated when a book on the shamrock by Charles Nelson of the National Botanic Gardens, Glasnevin, appears. Dr Nelson's botanical pronouncement on the shamrock, published in 1985, represents the current orthodox opinion on the question of its genus. 'In one sense,' writes Dr Nelson, 'there is no such thing as shamrock; no single uniquely Irish species can be equated with *seam rog*. In another sense, gardeners spend a fortune each year trying to eliminate it from their immaculate lawns, while farmers try to encourage it in their pastures. Shamrock is nothing more than clover.' More specifically, Dr Nelson explains that the shamrock is 'the winter resting stage of white or yellow clover (*Trifolium repens* or *Trifolium dubium*). When we gather shamrock the weather is still cold, and plants are in the resting stage, small-leaved and compact.' This is very close to the result obtained by Nathaniel Colgan in 1896 when he conducted a survey asking people to send him 'genuine shamrock' from all over Ireland. The vast majority of those who responded sent him yellow clover – *Trifolium dubium*.

At least nowadays we know which plant we are talking about. However, Colgan and subsequent writers fail to make what seems to me a very obvious connection between the history of the shamrock in the sixteenth century and its seventeenth-century development. In the late sixteenth century the shamrock, or 'shamrogue', is mentioned by English observers of Irish habits as an indication of their barbarousness. The Irish are so uncouth, English observers repeatedly tell us, that they eat shamrocks and other grasses that grow wild in ditches. 'Shamrock-eaters' quickly became a derogatory term for the Gaelic Irish. Yet, less than a century later, these same Gaelicized Irish are proudly displaying the shamrock in their hats while celebrating the feast day of their most famous saint.

This is surely an example of a symbol, chosen by the oppressor to designate inferiority and difference, being deliberately adopted by those whom it was meant to denigrate, as a positive symbol of their separate identity. The shamrock is a badge of identity which only the 'native Irish' would choose to wear with pride, thereby differentiating themselves from their Anglicized neighbours. There may have been other additional reasons why the shamrock was originally chosen as an emblem of Irishness, but this defiant gesture of pride in Irish identity was surely one of them.

A glance at some sixteenth-century references to the shamrock-eating Irish will illustrate the contempt in which they were held by the English. The most famous of all is a passage from the poet Edmund Spenser in which he describes the state of the rebel soldiers of Munster in the early 1580s following the Desmond rebellion:

> Ere one year and a half they were brought to such wretchedness as that any stony heart would have rued the same. Out of every corner of the woods and glens they came creeping forth upon their hands, for their legs could not bear them, they looked like anatomies of death, they spoke like ghosts, crying out of their graves, they did eat the dead carrions, happy where they could find them, yea, and one another soon after, insomuchas the very carcasses they spared not to scrape out of their graves and if they found a plot of watercresses or shamrocks, there they flocked as to a feast for a time, yet not being able to continue there withal, that in short space there were none almost left, and a most populous and plentiful country suddenly left void of man or beast.

Spenser's account is at least tempered by some humanitarian sympathy for those grotesque figures driven by starvation to eat corpses and 'feast' on shamrocks. One can detect no such sympathy in John Derricke's Preface to *Image of Ireland with a Discoverie of Wood Kearne*. Derricke, writing in 1581, is referring to wood kernes (lightly-armed Irish foot soldiers), the same poor souls that Spenser was writing about, when he admits: 'For in verie trothe my harte abhorreth their dealynges and my soul dooeth deteste their wilde shamrocke manners.'

Derricke's use of 'shamrocke' as an adjective denoting 'Irish' is an interesting linguistic shift, indicating that there was at the time a well-recognized association in the English mind between the shamrock and the native or 'mere' Irish.

Of all the habits peculiar to the Irish, it is hard to see why the eating of shamrock was singled out and viewed with such contempt by English observers. The Irish habit of shamrock-eating was so widely referred to in the late sixteenth and early seventeenth centuries, that it formed part of what Colgan refers to as 'the then common stock of English knowledge, or ignorance, as some may prefer to call it, of Irish manners and customs'.

The first mention of the shamrock among herbalists occurs in 1570, when the famous Dutch botanist Matthias de l'Obel mentions the Irish habit of grinding meal from trefoils and kneading it with butter to make trefoil cakes – shamrock bread. In 1571, Edmund Campion makes the following observation in his *Historie of Ireland*: 'Shamrotes, water cresses and other herbs they feed upon: oatmele and butter they cramme together.

Many early observers confuse shamrock eating with watercress eating. As any modern nutritionist could tell them, given the diet of milk, butter and oatmeal common among all but the most wealthy Irish in those days, this 'barbarous habit' probably saved millions of Irish people from perishing from scurvy and other diseases caused by vitamin deficiencies. The vitamin-laden potato, it must be remembered, did not become the staple diet of the Irish until the mid- or late seventeenth century.

There was perhaps some criticism of Irish husbandry implicit in Englishmen's disgust at the habit of eating shamrock. The shamrock was not cultivated, but grew wild, and needed no preparation before it could be consumed. The habit was part of the improvidence and fecklessness that the Elizabethans saw as characteristic of their neighbours. Fynes Morrison, secretary to the Lord Deputy Mountjoy, is not surprised nor even sympathetic when replying to a Bohemian baron who has complained about the lack not only of bread, but even oat cakes among the Irish. He explains the situation:

Yea, the wild Irish in times of greatest peace impute covetousness and base birth to him that hath any corne after Christmas, as if it were a point of nobility to consume all within these festival days. They willingly eat the herbe shamrock being of sharp taste which as they run and are chased to and fro they snatch like beasts out of the ditches.

Again the shamrock seems to have been confused with watercress, given the 'sharp taste' of the latter. Other writers confuse it with wood sorrel. English children eat wood sorrel to this day, and call it 'sour dabs'. Sorrel soup and sorrel sauce are considered delicacies. Sorrel was widely cultivated in England until the reign of Henry VIII as a salad.

Sir James Ware in *De Hibernia* (1654) describes the diet of the 'ancient Irish' (i.e., the Irish in Elizabethan times) as 'meagre – milk, butter and herbs for the most part – meadow trefoil, water cress, common sorrel and cochlearia'.

Cochlearia is better known by its vernacular name, scurvy grass. John Gerard, the sixteenth-century herbalist, tells us that 'this excellent plant Caesar's soldiers found to prevail against the plague and hurtful disease of the teeth, gums and sinewes', and Captain Cook carried it in dried bundles to prevent scurvy on his long sea voyages. It is neither a trefoil nor a grass, but it has a small heart-shaped leaf and spreads low over the ground so that, from a distance, it could easily be confused with watercress or even shamrock.

Between 1570 and 1680, therefore, there is no reference yet traced to the shamrock as anything but a food among the Irish. It is often the case that those living in a country find its peculiar habits and traditions too much a commonplace part of everyday life to be worthy of special comment, and such customs remain unrecorded until remarked upon by an outsider. This appears to have been the case with the shamrock's transition from food and symbol of uncouthness to emblem of Irishness and pride in that identity. For the first mention of the shamrock badge comes from the 1681 journal of an Englishman, one Thomas Dinely, who travelled in Ireland in the reign of Charles II: 'The 17th day of March yearly is Saint Patrick's, an immoveable feast when ye Irish of all stations and conditions wear crosses in their hats, some of pins, some of green ribbon, and the vulgar superstitiously wear shamroges, 3-leaved grass, which they likewise eat (they say) to cause a sweet breath.' Just how long the wearing of crosses and shamrocks on Saint Patrick's Day had been going on before Dinely observed it is not confirmed.

Another line of investigation into the apparently sudden appearance of the shamrock as the badge of Saint Patrick consists in looking at the appearance of shamrocks and the figure of Saint Patrick on coins. The evidence here strongly suggests that the association between Saint Patrick and the shamrock grew during precisely those years which saw the widespread suppression of the Catholic Irish and the large-scale confiscation of their lands.

Shamrocks had appeared on coins in much the same non-ideological, decorative way that they appeared on tiles or carved in stone from the twelfth century onwards. The first time that the shamrock was put into the hand of Saint Patrick, who offers it to the assembled people, was on coins issued by the Confederate Catholics of Kilkenny in 1645. The lowly herb was thus endowed with a whole new set of powerful symbolic associations.

In the years preceding the Confederation of Kilkenny (1642), land had been seized from both the Catholic Old Irish families of Ulster and the Catholic descendants of the Normans, the Old English. Large sections of both communities had refused to conform to the new Established Church, and remained faithful to Catholicism. Efforts to outlaw the old religion had been unsuccessful, and merely forced it temporarily underground. Old Irish and Old English joined forces as the 'Confederate Catholics' and set up an administration in Kilkenny, declaring that they were not up in arms against the king, but wished to secure their position by negotiation. Their demands were clear: the reversal of land plantations, which would return vast tracts of the country to Catholic ownership, and the freedom to practise the Roman Catholic religion without state interference.

In 1645 the mint of the papal nuncio Rinuccini, in the Catholic Confederate stronghold of Kilkenny, issued the coin mentioned above. On one side was a kneeling king playing a harp (the Confederates were Royalists), and on the other Saint Patrick, in contemporary mitre and crozier holding out a leaf of shamrock to the people. The coins became known as 'Saint Patrick's money'. Catholic Ireland, literally under siege, chose to represent its separateness from the rest of the Irish nation by dressing the saint who had brought Christianity to the island in robes which could be immediately recognized as those of a bishop, and putting into his hand a plant associated with the native Irish and, one can assume, by now also with Saint Patrick's teaching of the doctrine of the Trinity.

The extent to which the shamrock was associated, in the opposing English (and Protestant) tradition, during the seventeenth century with a derogatory view of Irishness can be judged from looking at a verse epic by James Farewell entitled *The Irish Hudibras* (1689). It is a satire based on the sixth book of the *Aeneid*. Colgan refers to it as 'this deservedly scarce work' and, a true Victorian gentleman, applies the standards of his age to those passages he wishes to quote by censoring certain lines.

It is an extraordinary poem, and remains to this day 'scarce'. It is not, as far as I can discover, available in any modern scholarly edition, and has to be read in its original 1689 edition in the National Library in Dublin. It is a facetious but vigorous work featuring a hero called Nees (Aeneas). Nees enters Hell through Saint Patrick's Purgatory in Lough Derg and meets the shades of the Irish heroes. The shamrock is substituted for the golden branch (*aureus ramus*) which smoothed Aeneas' passage from the underworld. So close is the connection between the shamrock and the Irish at this period that Ireland is spoken of throughout as 'Shamrogshire' and, in Colgan's words 'the mention of an Irishman seems just as naturally to suggest to the writer, thoughts of an Irishman's favourite food, the shamrock, as the word Frenchman was, at one time, wont to call up thoughts of stewed frogs in the minds of Englishmen.'

Thus when Nees, having anchored in Lough Erne, sends a mariner ashore in search of food, the mariner returns triumphantly with shamrock in hand:

Springs, happy springs, adorn'd with sallets [salads]
Which nature purposed for their Palats;
Shamroges and watercress he shows,
Which was both meat, and Drink and close.

The second line of the next quotation, a robust description of the shades of the Irish heroes in the underworld, was delicately omitted by Colgan:

Stalking about the bogs and moors
Together with their Dogs and Whores;
Without a Rag, Trouses or Brogues,
Picking of Sorrels and Sham-rogues.

The contemporary difference in the ideological perception of the shamrock between the Protestant (Established Church) Anglo-Irish tradition, as represented by Farewell, and the Catholic, Jacobite mind, is vividly illustrated by the fact that, during the siege of Limerick in 1690, the Jacobites issued a coin showing a figure emblematic of Ireland holding a shamrock. The Jacobite coin is especially important as it is an early example of the shamrock alone (i.e., not in the hand of Saint Patrick) being used in a symbolic attempt to represent Ireland.

Just how much superstition was associated with the shamrock can be judged from the following anonymous snippet which originated in America. Its language and the mention of emigration date it to the latter part of the nineteenth century, but its opening reference to 'olden times' suggests that it is describing beliefs current in the eighteenth century, beliefs which could well date from much earlier:

In olden times the shamrock was highly regarded as a defence against the malevolent power of witches. Irish peasants plucked the leaf before venturing across lonely moors where banshees wailed and fairies were wont to spirit away the souls of travellers, and many of its apotropaic powers are still believed in parts of Ireland. If a farmer plucks a sprig and takes it home, all will go well with his cattle on May Day. The colleen who surreptitiously conceals a leaf in the shoe of her departing lover can be certain of his return. When plucked with a gloved hand and carried secretly into a house where an insane person resides, the magical shamrock will cure the patient. Emigrants leaving Ireland commonly carry a sprig to ensure good luck.

There are, interestingly, no references at all in Irish folklore tradition to the shamrock as a food. Folk-memory of the bad times when shamrock formed part of the national diet seems to have died out completely. Nor is there any evidence in folk traditions of memories of a time when the shamrock was used by the English as a derogatory emblem of Irishness. This does not, however, invalidate my suggestion that one reason why the shamrock was displayed on Saint Patrick's Day could initially have been in defiance of those who identified the shamrock with the 'wilde Irish'. The memory of such a gesture, and also that of shamrock-eating, could die out within a generation.

Before the Norman invasion, the anniversary of Saint Patrick's 'falling asleep' was a three-day-long religious festival, with a lengthy sermon on the saint's glorious deeds as the highlight of each day's celebrations. By the seventeenth century, Saint Patrick's Day was, to judge by available records, celebrated in a far more secular manner. The same Thomas Dinely whose 1681 *Journal* first recorded the wearing of shamrocks on Saint Patrick's Day, made one further observation of that day's festivities: 'The common people and servants also demand their Patrick's groat of their masters, which they goe expressly to town, though half a dozen miles off, to spend . . . and very few of the zealous are found sober at night.'

This is the first specific historical record of a connection between drunkenness and the celebration of Saint Patrick's Day. There are, however, many records of complaints earlier in the seventeenth century of a general tendency among the Irish to combine the celebration of religious festivals and pilgrimages with prodigious bouts of drunkenness and debauchery, especially at 'patterns' (a corruption of 'patrons'), as the celebration of patron saints' days was known. The same sort of behaviour was observed at wakes.

Such drunkenness is a legacy of the Old Gaelic tradition of offering generous, even unstinting, hospitality to one's guests. Professor Patrick J. Corish of Maynooth, writing of the early seventeenth century, describes the official concern that resulted:

> There were many other social occasions [besides wakes], for the laity baptisms and marriages, for the clergy patronal feasts, where the bishops complained of excessive, indeed ruinous, expense on the provision of lavish food, drink and entertainment for the great crowds, clergy and laity, who were expected to come and came. It was not easy to change this practice, for it reflected a deeply-felt need to appear *flaithiúlach* [generous] in the eyes of one's peers.

Corish, in the same study, presents an interesting thesis, which I would suggest has great importance for the connection between Saint Patrick and the shamrock, when he suggests that there was a considerable growth in the belief in superstitions in the stressful years following Cromwell's ruthless suppression of Catholicism. In the 1650s, as in the 1620s, bishops were still complaining of the feasting and sexual licence associated with wakes, but the synods of the 1650s also mention their concern about the invocation of the devil, witchcraft, a proliferation of dubious relics, curing prayers, holy wells, pilgrimages and patterns. Note the inclusion of 'patterns' – boisterous celebration of patron saints' feast days in a manner peculiar to the Irish – in the list of superstitious usages.

Lough Derg seems to have been an exception to the general rule that religious pilgrimages, like patterns, provided an occasion for 'dancing, carousing and drinking'. The pilgrimages referred to were mostly small local ones to a holy well or other traditional shrine. Complaints of boisterous behaviour and worse – faction-fighting, even full-scale riots – among pilgrims can be found throughout the seventeenth and eighteenth centuries.

While the bishops were no doubt correct to complain of such

behaviour, it must be remembered that, for the seventeenth-century labourer or small farmer, religious holidays, baptisms, marriages and wakes were the only sort of holiday available, and also the only occasions which could justify a bout of conviviality. There were, of course, no such things as institutionalized national holidays. (Saint Patrick's Day was not made a national holiday until 1903 when a bill introduced by the Earl of Dunraven in the House of Lords was passed by the Westminster parliament.) The seventeenth- and eighteenth-century peasants found that even the traditional festivals associated with the agricultural calendar – *Samhain* and *Lughnasa*, for example – had been taken over by the church.

Saint Patrick's Day itself, as we can see from folkloric traditions, marked an important event in the farming year – the official start of spring. It was still referred to in the early twentieth century by country people as the day on which Saint Patrick takes the 'cold stone' out of the water – the stone which had been put in on Hallowe'en. It was also the date from which the sowing of the new crop could start.

There was, therefore, nothing in the annual calendar of the rural Irish to give cause for celebration except religious occasions. Besides Sundays, the only days off work were those on which something religious was to be celebrated – a marriage, a baptism, funeral, a pilgrimage to a local shrine, a saint's feast day or other church holiday. Little wonder then that, in a society which produced (at home and as yet untaxed) some of the best hard liquor in the world (*uisquebeaugh* – alias whiskey), once Mass and devotions were over, 'dancing, carousing and drinking' were the order of the day on religious holidays.

For all its brave efforts to survive violent oppression, the sort of Catholicism which the rural Irish peasantry practised in the seventeenth and eighteenth centuries was very different from the modern Catholicism shaped by the Council of Trent (1563). Catholicism as practised before the Council of Trent, pre-Tridentine Catholicism, persisted in rural Ireland long after it had been replaced by the new Catholicism elsewhere in Europe.

Ireland had its own very difficult problems when it came to the implementation of reforms. For a start, Catholics were forced to practise their religion clandestinely at several periods during the seventeenth and early eighteenth centuries. Diocesan and parochial organization of the outlawed church was badly disrupted. Illiteracy was widespread. Even after church reorganization in the later seventeenth century, and a brief period of religious tolerance, not all parish priests were as conscientious as they could have been in drilling the rudiments of the faith into their flock. Corish observes of these years that the level of personal commitment to Catholicism (i.e., knowledge of its dogma and observance of its rites) 'tends to decrease as one moves out from the towns and down the ranks of society'. Thus the rural poor, who were the most assiduous in their observation of traditional pilgrimages and patterns, and among whom superstitious practices were most prevalent, were in fact extremely ignorant (through no fault of their own) of standard post-Tridentine Catholicism.

Instead of improving in the eighteenth century, the situation worsened. Up until the 1730s Catholic priests were actively persecuted. It was during this period that the 'hedge-schools' came into existence, providing rural communities with an education of a kind, supposedly Catholic. It is a movement which has been much romanticized in recent years, and scholars are only now starting to examine just how widespread and efficacious hedge-schools actually were. However, as they existed to provide a Catholic and Irish education, one can safely assume that they contributed to the oral growth of the Saint Patrick legend.

Church reorganization following the penal years was a slow and cumbersome business. Tolerance of Catholic activity was often dependent on the attitude of the local landowner. In some areas chapels, or mass-houses as they were called, were permitted; in others Mass had to be said either on a 'mass-rock' in the open air, or, as in the seventeenth century, in private homes. Outside the towns, the humbler people's knowledge of the church's teaching depended almost entirely on the calibre and level of activity of their parish priest.

Not surprisingly, superstition continued to flourish. This extract from *The Good Confessor* (1743), which is proposed as useful for the examination of conscience before confession, shows how widespread superstitious habits were by the mid-eighteenth century:

> Did you make use of any superstitions, or vain observations, persuading yourself that there are lucky and unlucky days: unlucky if the first person you should meet in the morning should be red-haired, or if a hare should cross the way before you, or if a grave should be opened on a Tuesday, or if a marriage, or any bargain should be made on that day of the week, upon which Holy Innocents fell that year, or if thirteen should be at table, etc., which are the remains of heathenism, vain and groundless remarks?
>
> Did you make use of superstitious things for curing of diseases in men or cattle, which have, or can have, no natural connection with these effects, such as billets, certain words, prayers not approved by the Church, herbs gathered before sunrise, or on certain days only, a little stone, or flint-arrow dipped in milk, ale or water . . . had you recourse to magicians, sorcerers or witches?

In the early seventeenth century the clergy made some efforts to turn the celebration of pilgrimages and patterns into valid celebrations of Christian saints. As times grew harder for the church, such efforts seem to have slackened off, and the people (especially in rural areas) were more or less left to their own devices on these occasions. By the end of the eighteenth century, the now reorganized church had 'set its face against the tradition of pilgrimage and pattern, and thereby helped to ensure that they would degenerate into "meetings of pretended devotion, or rather of real dissipation and dissoluteness" ' (Corish).

Saint Patrick's Day was, of course, only one patron saint's feast day among many. Saints Brigid, Kevin, Colmcille, Declan, Ailbe, Ciaran and numerous lesser known local patrons were all honoured in a similar fashion – attendance at Mass, perhaps a pilgrimage to a holy well or some other spot locally associated with the saint, and then a good long bout of carousing. But Saint Patrick was, as the first bishop of Ireland and the man responsible for the conversion of the whole island, deserving of a bigger and better pattern than anyone else. One can safely assume that devotion to Saint Patrick was greater in those areas which had strong traditional associations with the saint – Armagh, Downpatrick, Saul, Murrisk, Aghagower and so on – but by the early eighteenth century the celebration of Saint Patrick's Day by attendance at Mass, informal parading in the streets wearing ribbons or shamrock, and the imbibing of strong liquor had become a nation-wide custom.

If we look back again to the first mention of the wearing of the green, Thomas Dinely's *Journal* for 1681 (see above, pp. 114–15), two points will now emerge as being of especial significance. The first is his distinction between 'ye Irish *of all stations and conditions*' (my italics) who wear crosses and pins or green ribbons in their hats, and the *'vulgar'* who 'superstitiously wear shamrogues'. The second point is that he does not mention general drunkenness, but only accuses 'the common people and servants' of this indulgence – presumably the same class as those he has earlier called the 'vulgar'.

Dinely's connection between shamrock wearing and the lower social orders is corroborated by later writers, as is his connection between this same social stratum and drunkenness on Saint Patrick's Day. The botanist Caleb Threlkeld, whom we have already quoted as giving the earliest known literary expression to the notion that Saint Patrick used the shamrock to explain the Trinity (1727), adds that '. . . when they wet their seamar-oge [shamrock], they often commit excess in liquor, which is not a right keeping of a day to the Lord; error generally leading to debauchery.'

Jonathan Swift, writing in his 1713 *Journal* to Stella, gives an incidental insight into the observation of Saint Patrick's Day in London at that date: 'The Irish folks were disappointed that the Parliament did not meet today because it was Saint Patrick's Day, and the Mall was so full of crosses that I thought all the world was Irish.' This is the earliest evidence we have for the observance of Saint Patrick's Day outside Ireland by Irish people other than the military. It seems that, even in 1713, the exiles put on a numerically impressive show.

Because Swift does not mention the wearing of shamrocks,

Nathaniel Colgan concludes that it must have been popular at a later date. However, Swift was observing wealthy, city people who frequented the newly fashionable West End of London. Given Dinely's evidence (1681), I would suggest that Swift's remarks confirm my own theory that the wearing of the shamrock on Saint Patrick's Day originated among the Irish peasantry. Why spend money, of which there was very little, on a ribbon, when you have Saint Patrick's own plant growing outside your cabin door?

Those who chose to display the shamrock, therefore, were the same people whose behaviour at patterns and pilgrimages caused such concern to the bishops throughout the seventeenth and eighteenth centuries: those at the very bottom of the social scale, more often rural than urban dwellers, whose circumstances caused them to remain largely ignorant of the true nature of Catholicism and dependent on a large body of superstition inherited from their 'heathen' past. Yet their very ignorance and isolation allowed them to remain closer, albeit unconsciously, to the traditions of their Gaelic past than did their better educated and more sophisticated urban neighbours.

Dinely specifically mentions green ribbons, but the next reference we have to Saint Patrick's Day badges, made in 1682, remarks that Irish troops quartered in a town in England, wore red ribbons in their hats 'after their country manner' on 17 March.

The red saltire of Saint Patrick is the official emblem for Ireland in British heraldry. This is the diagonal red cross which has, since the Act of Union in 1801, stood in the Union Flag as the symbol of Ireland under the red cross of Saint George and superimposed on the white saltire of Saint Andrew. There has been much discussion, often distorted by anti-British sentiment, about the antiquity of the red saltire of Saint Patrick.

Although there is some evidence for a traditional association between Saint Patrick and the red saltire before the eighteenth century, it was not officially associated with him until 1783 when the Order of the Knights of Saint Patrick was instituted. The close associations between this order and the oligarchy of the time, the Protestant Ascendancy, has led subsequent historians to deny the existence of any previous links between Saint

Patrick and the saltire. Their argument claims that the device was borrowed from the arms of the FitzGerald family – the Earls of Kildare and Desmond – in the absence of any traditional Patrician heraldic device. Others argue that the red saltire has a longer and more authentic history as a national device. A flag bearing the red saltire was carried by the Catholic Confederates (the same people who minted the first coin bearing Saint Patrick and a shamrock) in 1644. A saltire appears in the arms of Trinity College in 1612. Most significantly, as far as a connection between the cross and Saint Patrick is concerned, it also features on the old seal of the Dean and Chapter of Armagh.

The use of red crosses by the military to denote Irishness in 1682 would tend to confirm the antiquity of the red saltire's association with Saint Patrick. It seems not unlikely, therefore, that during the seventeenth century the red Saint Patrick's cross was deemed acceptable as a device signifying Irishness. At some point during the eighteenth century the red of the saltire became unpopular and was replaced by green. The respectable Volunteer Movement of 1778 used shamrock as an emblem. In 1798 the insurgents led by Wolfe Tone and his United Irishmen chose to rise up under a green flag – the old nationalist banner of an uncrowned gold harp on a green ground.

The uprisings were a disaster, not only in terms of military defeat and loss of life but also politically. They led to a mood of panic which was shared by the Ascendancy, who feared for their ability to maintain their position as an oligarchy; the Catholic hierarchy, who feared the introduction into Ireland of the godless ideals of French republicanism; and the English government, who feared for their ability to retain control over the neighbouring island. Collusion between these three elements led to the Act of Union. On New Year's Day 1801, Ireland became part of the United Kingdom of Britain and Ireland. The Dublin parliament was dissolved and Irish members took their seats at Westminster.

This political development, which was abhorred by the vast majority of the Irish people, was expressed symbolically by adding the red saltire of Saint Patrick to the British flag. Little wonder, then, that red crosses were no longer displayed by the Irish on Saint Patrick's Day.

That same red saltire had already been appropriated, as we have mentioned, in 1783, as part of the regalia of the Order of the Knights of Saint Patrick. It is significant that this short-lived heraldic order, which existed to bestow honour and a sense of importance on members of the Ascendancy, chose for its flag a gold harp on a pale blue ground. Because of this, the official colour of Saint Patrick in heraldry is pale blue. There are reasons for believing that the red saltire at one time had genuine associations of some antiquity with Saint Patrick. In contrast, the introduction of pale blue into Patrician symbolism has never been popularly accepted. Shamrock green remained the colour of Saint Patrick for the great majority of the Irish people.

It is possible to make many conjectures about why green was adopted as the national colour. There is no doubt that its association with Saint Patrick and the shamrock in the minds of the people of Ireland played a large part in the process. Perhaps the best of the other explanations for the origin of the national colour is also the simplest: Ireland is a very green country. Green reminds the exile of home. Green is also a usefully symbolic colour in itself, quite apart from its associations with Ireland.

Consider the following figurative qualities of green as listed by the *Shorter Oxford English Dictionary*:

1. Full of vitality; not withered or worn out. 2. Of tender age, youthful. 3. Unripe, immature, undeveloped. Raw, untrained, inexperienced. 4. That has not been prepared by drying; hence, not ready for use or consumption. 5. Unaltered by time or natural processes; fresh, new.

A more apt colour to accompany the emergence of a new nation simply could not be found.

It is not surprising, therefore, that green, which had already been established as a badge of Irishness worn on the patron saint's feast day, should be adopted by the aspiring nationalist movements which emerged in Ireland towards the end of the eighteenth century, and eventually be represented in the official flag of the independent Republic of Ireland, the tricolour.

The harsh punishment meted out to the nationalists who had fought under the green banner, and widespread dissatisfaction at

the Union with England, produced a series of rousing patriotic
ballads, which circulated in broadsheets. This was Ireland's first
crop of rebel songs, and many of them are sung with enthusiasm
to this day. One of the most famous Irish songs of all, 'The Wearing of the Green', is believed by many people to date from
this period. The best-known version, however, was written by
the playwright Dion Boucicault in the mid-nineteenth century.
The 'law' it mentions was applied to Irish regiments in Queen
Victoria's time, and forbade them to wear shamrock in the – by
then traditional – Saint Patrick's Day parade. It demonstrates
how completely Saint Patrick, the shamrock, the colour green
and nationalist sentiment were fused together in the popular
imagination:

Oh Paddy dear and did you hear the news that's going round,
The shamrock is forbid by law to grow on Irish ground.
No more Saint Patrick's Day we'll keep, his colours can't be
    seen.
For there's a cruel law against the Wearing of the Green.

I met with Napper Tandy and he took me by the hand
And he said, 'How's poor old Ireland and how does she
    stand?'
She's the most distressful country that ever yet was seen
For they're hanging men an' women for the Wearing of the
    Green.

And if the colour we must wear is England's cruel red,
Let it remind us of the blood that Ireland has shed;
Then pull the shamrock from your hat, and throw it on the
    sod,
And never fear, 'twill take root there, though under foot 'tis
    trod.

When law can stop the blades of grass from growin' as they
    grow.
And when the leaves in summer time their colour dare not
    show,
Then I will change the colour, too, I wear in my *caubeen*;
But till that day, please God, I'll stick to the Wearing of the
    Green.

7
SAINT PATRICK'S DAY

Saint Patrick's Day is often an anti-climax for the thousands of Irish-Americans who choose to spend 17 March in Ireland. Although, largely for their benefit, the Irish Tourist Board organizes an American-style Saint Patrick's Day parade in Dublin, elsewhere in the country it is a quiet, low-key holiday. In Kinsale, where I live, many people go to Mass, everyone puts on their Sunday best and convivial spirits congregate in the pub at lunchtime: in 1987, for the first time, some of the pubs served green beer. It is the final meet of the season for the local hunt. As a child I was usually taken to a simple after-Mass parade held in a neighbouring village, Carrigaline, featuring the Ballinhassig Pipe Band. The parade in the nearest city, Cork, is under threat from lack of commercial sponsorship; not many people from Kinsale bother to attend.

Most people wear shamrock, either picked by themselves or bought from the travelling people on the streets of Cork city, although a few people, mainly children, prefer commercially manufactured favours – green, white and orange ribbons with a plastic harp, and the like. Some people make a special point of cooking traditional fare such as bacon and cabbage, or crubeens (pickled pig's trotters), but there are few parties, and no organized events except perhaps a dance or a Saint Patrick's Disco in the evening. Some other small towns still retain a tradition of amateur dramatic performances on Saint Patrick's Day, a tradition fostered by the clergy in the late nineteenth and early twentieth centuries, when the prohibition on dancing and the consumption of alcohol during Lent was strictly enforced. Nowadays many people who have given up drink for Lent allow themselves a dispensation on 17 March in honour of the saint. It is a busy day in the bars.

I have spent as many Saint Patrick's Days in London as I have in Ireland, and it is my experience that it is far easier to have a good time on that day outside Ireland than it is at home. Abroad one has a certain novelty value as a genuine 'Paddy'. Most Irish journalists would agree that, when Fleet Street still existed, it was virtually impossible to get any work done on 17 March, so numerous and pressing were the invitations to have a drink. Outside Ireland there is a compulsion to 'show the flag' and be seen to be celebrating on Saint Patrick's Day which does not exist at home. At home, ironically, it still feels like a new Bank Holiday, held at an awkward time of year, on which, unless you intend to get well and truly plastered, or stay slumped in front of the television absorbing the relentlessly Irish flavour which dominates the day's programming, it is difficult to think of anything much to do. Parades are usually over by lunchtime, and the weather is often too cold to stay out for much longer. The pubs are packed with noisy drunks, and as the evening wears on they will start to sing sentimental ballads off-key. A bottle of whiskey beside your own fire and a few friends to share it with seems the best option.

I look on 17 March as the date by which, in a good year, the daffodils should be out. The local farmers still pride themselves on finishing the ploughing and the harrowing before 'Paddy's Day', and wait until it is over to set their potatoes. Up until the 1930s or so, it used to be the custom in rural areas for the father of the house to take a charred stick from the fire and make a cross with it on the children's shoulders. The practice has died out, and its origins are unknown: it may have begun in penal times, when Catholicism was outlawed in Ireland, to provide a secret badge and reminder of a family's adherence to the faith.

Most of the traditional Saint Patrick's Day pilgrimages have also been abandoned. One such small 'pilgrimage', which took place without the presence of the clergy, is remembered by the poet Desmond O'Grady (b. 1935). As a child he used to accompany his mother on a particular circuitous route across the fields outside Limerick every Saint Patrick's Day, stopping to pray at prescribed places – 'doing the stations'. A picnic, the first of the year, was the high spot of the day for him, while his mother enjoyed the opportunity to pay social calls on her more remote neighbours, all of whom held open house for the occasion. As far as O'Grady can ascertain, the pilgrimage has now died out.

The Dublin parade dates from the early 1970s, and is regarded with suspicion as being unauthentic. Many of the participants are prize-winning American bands. An estimated 250,000 people attend the parade each year, and there are more than 5000 participants: a small event by American standards. The parade is watched by dignitaries from a reviewing stand opposite the famous General Post Office in O'Connell Street – the Lord Mayor of Dublin, the Leader of the Opposition, the director-general of the Tourist Board and so on. But the really important people – the Prime Minister, for example – are elsewhere: bestowing their presence on America's biggest Saint Patrick's Day parade in Manhattan.

The Irish at home may have reservations about the Americanization of the Dublin parade, but the Irish in America have no hesitation in using Saint Patrick's Day parades to encourage Americans to visit Ireland. The Irish Tourist Board, Aer Lingus, CIE Tours International (the Irish train and bus service) and the two main Irish banks are all major sponsors of the big Manhattan parade. Saint Patrick's Day is, of course, the highlight of the year for the overseas offices of the Irish Tourist Board, and no expense is spared in offering lavish Irish hospitality to local dignitaries and press, always, of course, with a view to promoting Ireland's all-important tourist industry.

The Dublin parade pales into insignificance compared with the thousands of Saint Patrick's Day celebrations held on American soil. The Americans' enthusiasm for celebrating Saint Patrick's Day, their initiative and their powers of organization, have done more to keep the observance of his feast day alive than anything done by the Irish at home. In Ireland we affect a certain superiority when we complain about the gaudiness and the naïvety of the American celebrations. But there is no doubt that such celebrations have genuine Irish roots. The traditional American celebrations of Saint Patrick's Day are much more closely linked to the Irish peasantry's pre-twentieth-century observance of Saint Patrick's Day than most Irish people will admit.

A brief look at the greetings card industry will illustrate this point. Saint Patrick's Day fills a convenient gap in the card shops between Saint Valentine's Day and Easter. About 15 million Saint Patrick's Day cards are sent annually in the in the USA,[1] and the custom is catching on fast in Ireland. An Post, the Irish postal service, introduced an annual collection of specially priced postage-paid Saint Patrick's Day cards in 1984, a service which is so popular that it sells an average of 1.7 million cards a year.

There is a marked split in the sort of cards available in Ireland, with the traditional sentimental cards rapidly losing ground to ribald humorous ones. The former will usually carry either an idyllic picture of green Irish countryside, or a picture of Saint Patrick as a bearded bishop with sixteenth-century robes, mitre and crozier, snakes under his foot and shamrocks for a border, with a rhyming message inside of which this, alas, is a typical example:

> May the blessings of Saint Patrick
> Be yours throughout the year;
> May his symbol of the shamrock
> To you be ever dear.
>
> (EuroGreetings – Made in Ireland)

No wonder the vast majority of urban sophisticates have no time for their patron saint. Such people, if they send a card at all, would no doubt choose a modern-looking, non-religious card such as the one with a greeen-suited leprechaun looking puzzled on the front and the words 'HAPPY SAINT PATRICK'S DAY! Say, do you know the difference between dancing an Irish jig and making love??? . . . You don't??!?' – And inside a leering leprechaun's face beneath the words '. . . May I have the next dance?' (Rustcraft Cards – Made in England).

Another common sentiment in the green greetings card business is expressed by a card which pictures on the front a wild party of green-dressed men and women in leprechaun hats getting outrageously drunk on green pints of beer with the words: 'On Saint Patrick's Day it's foolish for you to drink, overindulge and carry on into the wee hours of the night when you have to get up early the next day and go to work! So when you go out and celebrate be sensible . . .' And inside the message: 'Don't go to work the next day! Happy Saint Patrick's Day!' (Hallmark Cards – Made in USA).

Such cards, far from being a tasteless travesty of a religious holiday, contain a modern version of the spirit of the eighteenth-century Irish patterns, celebrations which were characterized by drunkenness, bawdiness and 'riotous behaviour'. This was the traditional way in which the rural Irish observed the feast day of their patron saint. It travelled to America with the nineteenth-century immigrants. It is a far more genuinely native tradition of the Irish people than the pious sentimentality of the shamrock-and-bishop cards. Yet most people are unaware of the origins of such boisterousness and dismiss these productions as a vulgar commercialization of the national holiday, attributable to American influence. In this case, the Americans are most definitely not guilty.

While figures for emigration from Ireland were high for the whole of the nineteenth century, they reached their peak in the years before and after the Great Famine of 1845. Significantly for the spread of the cult of Saint Patrick, those who left during these years came, by and large, from the same social class which was instrumental in elevating Saint Patrick and the shamrock to the status of national symbols – the rural poor. It was the picture of Saint Patrick as national hero, a grey-bearded man in green bishop's robes with the expelled serpents writhing at his feet and a border of shamrocks, whose anniversary must be given a boisterous and showy celebration on 17 March, that these emigrants took with them across the sea.

Between 1801 and 1921 over eight million men, women and children left Ireland, a figure which is equivalent to the entire population of Ireland at its peak, just before the Great Famine. Well over two-thirds of the emigrants headed for the United

States, where the majority of them settled in the great 'Irish' cities of New York, Boston, Philadelphia and Chicago.

These nineteenth-century emigrants who carried their nationalist sentiments and their devotion to Saint Patrick across the Atlantic were not, however, the first Irish people to move to the New World. From the early eighteenth century there had been a steady movement across the Atlantic of a rather different kind of person. While the vast majority of nineteenth-century immigrants were impoverished Catholics from rural districts seeking employment as servants and labourers, eighteenth-century immigrants in America were mainly relatively prosperous Ulster Protestants – farmers or merchants – who wished to contribute their skills to the colonization of the New World. They were also, in some cases, seeking an atmosphere which would be more tolerant of their Protestantism than Ulster. Before the American War of Independence, Catholics were not welcome in the Crown Colonies, unless they happened to be very wealthy.[2]

So it is a rather ironic fact of history, given that Saint Patrick is so closely associated with Catholic America these days, that the first recorded festivities and Friendly Societies associated with the saint in the New World were founded by Protestants; in some cases Catholics were specifically barred from participation.[3]

The first recorded meeting of Irishmen on American soil in honour of Saint Patrick took place in Boston on 17 March 1737. Presumably there were informal celebrations among private individuals before that date, but as yet no record of them has emerged. The 1737 meeting has come down to us in history because the gentlemen assembled on that occasion formed themselves into the Charitable Irish Society, whose aim was to provide assistance for their fellow-countrymen in those parts who were in economic difficulties. Their Rules and Orders at that date stipulated: '. . . the managers to be natives of Ireland or natives of any other part of the British dominion of Irish extraction, being Protestants and inhabitants of Boston.' However, the bar on Catholic membership of the Charitable Irish Society was either quickly repealed, or simply ignored, as Catholic gentlemen were to be found in the Society by 1742.

The fact that 17 March was chosen for the founding of the Charitable Irish Society indicated that the Irish immigrants in America, even at this early date, observed the feast of their patron saint. Not all the Irish in America at this time, however, were immigrants. During the lean years of the eighteenth century and the enforcement of the Penal Laws, many Irishmen chose to seek a military career abroad. Some joined the Catholic armies of France, Austria and Spain. Others found themselves in the English army, and a significant number of Irish, both officers and men, were subsequently posted to the colonies. They were to play an important part in establishing the American tradition of Saint Patrick's Day celebrations.

The earliest mention of military observance of Saint Patrick's Day in America – 17 March 1757 – does not, however, feature a parade. Instead it is the other aspect of secular Patrician festivities that is mentioned: the drowning of the shamrock.

It was the custom for the English army to issue an extra ration of grog on 17 March, in which to 'drown the shamrock'. In 1757, during the Seven Years War, the English troops were camped at Fort Henry, forty miles from the French stronghold of Ticonderoga. The English garrison consisted largely of Irishmen – so, by an odd twist of history, did the French contingent. The English troops, provincial rangers under John Stark, were issued with their extra rations of grog for shamrock-drowning on 16 March, as they were wary of a French attack on the next day. The French did indeed attack on 17 March, the Irish among them hoping that the Irish among the English would be taken unaware in a 'groggy' state. John Stark's precaution ensured that his troops were fully alert on 17 March, and the French attack was repulsed.

That the drowning of the shamrock was already associated with overindulgence in liquor in mid-eighteenth-century America is apparent from another military reference. Captain S. Ecuyer, in command of Fort Pitt (Pittsburgh) is writing to one Colonel Boquet on 18 March 1763. His Irish colleague was, it seems, under the weather on that day. Captain Ecuyer explains: 'We had Saint Patrick's fêtes in every manner so that Goghan could not write by this express.'

The first Saint Patrick's Day parade on record was held in New York in 1762, a year before Goghan's incapacitating hangover, and seems to have been a spontaneous event arising from the high spirits of a group of militia men. They were on their way to a Saint Patrick's Day breakfast at a tavern on Lower Broadway in New York City, and decided to march there behind their band with their regimental banners on display. The sight delighted participants and spectators in equal measure, and marching on 17 March to the rhythm of bands playing Irish tunes became a part of the American way of life.

Before marching caught on in a big way, Saint Patrick's Day was celebrated by 'breakfasts' – which were held at around 2 p.m. – in local taverns. Some of these were private affairs; others were hosted by Friendly Societies, like the aforementioned Irish Charitable Society, in which Irish immigrants banded together to help their less fortunate brothers, and also to enjoy each other's company.

The main feature of these breakfasts was the drinking of apparently interminable (and, alas, all too often incomprehensible) toasts. Raising a glass to 40 or 50 toasts at one sitting was not unusual, so it can be safely assumed that the participants were not destined to end the afternoon in a state resembling anything like sobriety. There were toasts to Saint Patrick and Ireland, but more popular in this early period were jocular and often rather sophisticated toasts concerned with the politics and gossip of the day – hence the difficulty a modern reader has in understanding their significance.

In the nineteenth century, after the execution of the leaders of the 1798 uprising and the Union with England these toasts became increasingly partisan, even inflammatory in tone. But in 1766 the healths drunk at a Saint Patrick's Day breakfast still reflected the loyalty to the Crown of the Protestant element, which continued to be dominant among the Irish in America. 'Saint Patrick's Day,' says a contemporary (1766) *Gazette*, 'was ushered in with fife and drums which produced a very agreeable harmony before the doors of many gentlemen of that [Irish] Nation and others.' A modest 20 toasts were drunk at the breakfast described by the *Gazette*, among them:

'The King and the Royal House of Hanover.'
'The Protestant Interest.'
'Mr Pitt.'
'May all Acts of Parliament contrary to the American Inter-
est be laid aside.'
'May the true sons of Liberty never want Roast Beef or
Claret.'
'The Lord Lieutenant of Ireland.'
'The Day, and Prosperity to Ireland.'
'May the enemies of Ireland never eat the Bread nor drink
the Whiskey of it, but be tormented with Itching without
the benefit of Scratching.'

Only three of the toasts mention Ireland, and apart from 'the day'
there is no reference at all to the saint who gave the occasion its
raison d'être.

During the War of Independence there is plenty of evidence
for the continuation of the tradition of military celebrations on
17 March. The date has a specific significance for Boston, as it
was on 17 March 1776 that the British evacuated the city, and the
American rebels, led by George Washington, took possession.

Washington was a great upholder of Saint Patrick's Day
festivities. The Day was celebrated in 1778 by his army at Valley
Forge, and the celebration marked the first occasion in American
history of racial tension on 17 March. The Irish were provoked
and, naturally enough, they fought back. Washington himself
had to intervene and make peace among the men. He then distributed extra rations of grog and declared 'I, too, am a lover of
Saint Patrick's Day.'

There are records of celebrations on 17 March throughout the
1770s and 1780s in New York and Boston, mostly taking the
form of breakfasts and balls hosted by Friendly Societies, and
military marches. One company of militia at least, Rawdon's
Volunteers, took advantage of the fine figure that they cut on the
patron saint's feast day for recruiting. Lord Rawdon, an Irish-
born veteran of Bunker Hill, raised a company called the Volunteers of Ireland who were quartered at Jamaica, Long Island.

Rivington's Gazette carried a long and flattering report on their turn-out in 1779 which concluded: 'The soldierly appearance of the men, their Order of March, Hand in Hand, being all Natives of Ireland, had a striking Effect; and many of their countrymen have since joined them.'

Many of the Irish Friendly Societies suspended their meetings between 1775 and 1784 on account of the War of Independence. Many others were founded immediately after Independence, for example, the Society of the Friendly Sons of Saint Patrick, which was formed in New York in 1784. They described themselves as 'a benevolent and patriotic society of Irishmen and their descendants of every shade of political and religious belief', which was founded 'to assist unfortunate and distressed natives of Ireland in the city of New York'. Little did they know just how many of these were to appear over the next 100 years.

It is not until the 1830s that the rural Catholic Irish began to arrive in the New World in great numbers and put their stamp upon the character of Saint Patrick's Day festivities. Before then, Irish-Scots – Presbyterians from Ulster – and their descendants dominated the Saint Patrick's Day celebrations which had a quite different atmosphere. These were not occasions of mass festivities, but exclusive balls and breakfasts for the upper social classes. Saint Patrick was a remote figurehead who provided an excuse for sophisticated socializing and the drinking of toasts to the health of the English government of Ireland. The less prosperous must also have had ways of celebrating Saint Patrick's Day – the army's extra ration of grog presumably had its civilian equivalent – but there are no records of them. It is also likely that the custom of providing servants and labourers with a gratuity on their saint's feast day crossed the Atlantic, along with the custom of wearing shamrock if obtainable (it took at least six weeks to make the crossing by ship, and was consequently dried or 'weathered') or something green instead.

By the early nineteenth century the Irish Americans were evolving a flamboyant style of expressing their allegiances symbolically, creating an iconography which would raise eyebrows and perhaps even fists back in the 'auld country'. Consider the

decor amidst which the Friendly Sons of Saint Patrick chose to
dine at the Bank Coffee House in New York City on 17 March
1828:

> . . . Saint Patrick in a Bishop's costume, on either side flags of
> Ireland and the USA, banners of Saint George and Saint
> Andrew, and sundry insignia of Brian Boru. An arch and
> columns at the other end of the room were decorated with
> various flags and the following names: Sterne, Swift, Burke,
> Sheridan, Montgomery, Grattan, Moore, Curran . . . with two
> banners in mourning: Clinton [De Witt Clinton, Mayor of
> New York, recently deceased and a member of the Society]
> and Emmet, the whole surmounted by an eagle with extended
> wings uniting the Irish harp and the shield of the United
> States of America, an olive branch and a bunch of arrows in its
> claws, a garland of shamrock in its mouth. The ceiling and
> sides of the room were hung with festoons of green, blue, red
> and white bunting. Over the head of Patrick on a green ground
> were the words *Erin Go Bragh* [Ireland Forever].

From 1801 onwards the toasts drunk by Irish Americans on
Saint Patrick's Day became increasingly political. They demonstrate that the predilection shown by certain Irish-Americans for
meddling in the internal affairs of modern Ireland is a very old
tradition, dating from the birth of the United States of America.

On reconvening the Charitable Irish Society of Boston in 1784,
its President declared: '. . . we have conquered one of the greatest
and most potent Nations on the Globe so far as to have peace and
Independency. May our friends, Countrymen of Ireland, Behave
like the brave Americans till they recover their Liberties.' In 1802
(a year after the Act of Union) the Hibernian Provident Society of
New York found a new symbolic use for the shamrock and drank
a toast to 'The 3 leaved shamrock of Ireland – May it ever remind
republicans of the 3 theological virtues, Faith, Hope and Charity,
imperative of their duty to relieve a republican in distress
and ameliorate his situation.' By 1812 they were drinking to:
'Ireland. A total separation from Britain, the sure mode of
emancipation: repeal of partial grievances only retards her

independence.' In 1833 the same Friendly Sons of Saint Patrick who had excelled themselves in patriotic decor at their 1828 festivities, were drinking to:

'Ireland – may she yet obtain a nationality.'
'Ireland – though burthened not disheartened.'
'The Star Spangled Banner – may a flag with the same liberty soon wave over the green island of Erin.'

The tradition of organizing a Saint Patrick's Day parade established itself throughout the United States of America in the nineteenth century. New York claims to have held the first parade in 1762, and Boston initiated its parade in 1812. By the late 1860s about a dozen cities were holding large Saint Patrick's Day parades. Not all were peaceful affairs. In the late eighteenth and early nineteenth centuries non-Irish Americans took to mocking the Irish by displaying a 'stuffed Paddy' on the route: even at this early date, 'Paddy' was a recognized synonym for 'Irish'. The effigies were intended as insults, and the display of stuffed Paddies often coincided with a large influx of unskilled Irish immigrants to a particular area. A ban on burning effigies of Saint Patrick was declared in 1803, the year that gave Catholics of New York State the vote.

Displays of anti-Irish prejudice were to become common feature, not only of Saint Patrick's Day celebrations but of the everyday life of Irish immigrants, as the century progressed and the influx of job-seeking immigrants grew. Although the majority of the new immigrants came from a rural background, they preferred for the most part to settle in urban districts. Neighbourliness has always been a feature of rural Irish life, and the countryside that the immigrants had left behind was a densely populated one. The vast, underpopulated farming areas of the Midwest held little attraction for the rural Irish. Even the few who possessed the necessary agricultural skills (most of them 'farmed' little more than potatoes) found the isolation of American farms difficult to cope with.

It was the popular Saint Patrick of oral tradition, a hero of folktale as much as a Christian saint, the figure recently chosen as one of the symbols of the nationhood to which Ireland was aspiring, who was exported to America in the nineteenth century. He was regarded as much with simple affection as respect. The feast of Saint Patrick, or 'Paddy', was already established as the biggest and best 'pattern' of all, a day when religious devotions would be followed by secular entertainments including the consumption of quantities of hard liquor and subsequent undecorous behaviour. The immigrants, it would seem, saw no reason to tone down the exuberance of their observance of Saint Patrick's Day once they reached America.

Unfortunately, until the Saint Patrick's Day parades came to be organized by Friendly Societies and fraternities such as the Ancient Order of Hibernians in the mid-nineteenth century, there are scarcely any records of what went on at them. However, we have seen that even the gatherings of the wealthy, Protestant Irish-Americans were characterized by 'hilarity' and large-scale consumption of liquor, so it is only reasonable to assume that the large numbers of predominately young, unmarried Catholic immigrants would add an even more boisterous mood to the festivities.

The Irish were unusual among immigrant groups in several ways. They had the great advantage, in most cases, of a knowledge of English. They tended to be young, and to emigrate unmarried, with the sexes fairly evenly distributed. Thus they faced their new life not only without parental or community control in the matter of morals, but also without elders to uphold and pass on the community's tradition. What they had was each other, and their often nominal and passive allegiance to the Catholic church. Also, unlike other immigrant groups, once the Irish had left their native land, they were most unlikely to return. A survey has shown that for every 100 Irish emigrants only about 6 returned from the United States, compared with 12 English, 22 German or 58 Italian settlers. Contact with Ireland was, however, kept alive through letters and through songs and ballads of sentimental yearning for the green fields far away.

The immigrants of the famine years were exiles not for a better way of life (as were those who came before and after them), but simply for survival. Their longing for home turned into a virtual cult of homesickness, which was sentimentalized in popular culture, by songs such as this one:

Oh fare thee well Ireland, my own dear native land,
It breaks my heart to see friends part for it's then that the
tear drops fall.
I'm on my way to Amerikay, will I ere see my home once
more,
For now I leave my own true love on Paddy's Green
Shamrock Shore.

Saint Patrick's Day provided a perfect occasion for the whole community to lament together for their lost homeland and shed a few maudlin but no doubt therapeutic tears.

It is no great wonder, then, that those generations of Irish immigrants who lacked a background of family elders and did not, owing to their youth and minimal education, have a great deal of knowledge about the country that they had left, seized upon the one thing that they all remembered from home – Saint Patrick's Day – as the occasion on which, literally, to parade their Irishness, and join together in celebrating their difference from their neighbours. At home it had been enough to walk to and from Mass wearing a sprig of shamrock. In America, something green was a lot cheaper than imported shamrock. The military example had shown the effectiveness of marching behind a band that was playing Irish airs – a spectacle enjoyed as much by the non-Irish as the Irish. Put the two together – parading in green along the street and the playing of rousing, melodic music – and the result is an enjoyable occasion of patriotic self-indulgence economically accessible to even the poorest of the community.

It was not until the turn of the century that the Saint Patrick's Day parade became an accepted part of the American way of life. The influx of hard-working young Irish people to the newly industrialized urban areas before, during and after the famine years, provoked resentment among the native population. The Irish were accused of taking jobs away from native Americans and of bringing down wages by being prepared to work for less than other people. Those who could not, for whatever reason, find work were accused of being a burden on the welfare agencies. Their rural ways and difference in matters of dress and speech further fuelled prejudice. But what really scared the 'nativists', as the anti-immigrationists became known, was the religion of the newcomers. Immigration before and after the famine introduced Catholicism into America on a hitherto unknown scale. In 1851, for example, the peak year of emigration, some 260,000 Irish immigrants, nearly all of the Catholic religion, arrived in the United States.

The nativists were not slow to organize against the newcomers. In 1834 the Ursuline Convent in Boston was burned to the ground by an organization called the American Protective Association. Job discrimination and physical attacks on Catholics (German as well as Irish) were commonplace.

The increase in anti-Catholic violence led to the establishment of the Ancient Order of Hibernians in New York in 1836. The Order was founded in Ireland in 1520, and the reason for its existence in America was the same as it had been originally: 'To protect the Mass, the priest and the Church.' There was intense anti-Catholic activity in America's new cities in the period 1844–56. The Ancient Order of Hibernians grew greatly in numbers over these years, thanks to the large number of Irish immigrants who continued to arrive and the increased prosperity of the earlier immigrants, as well as constant threats from nativist groups. In 1853 the Ancient Order of Hibernians took over the organization of the Saint Patrick's Day parade in New York City. It is still the organizing body of Manhattan's annual parade, the biggest and most famous of them all.

Not all Irish-Americans chose to celebrate Saint Patrick's Day in the latter half of the nineteenth century. During the Civil War the Irish took the largest number of losses among any ethnic group. Because so many Irish had died for their new country, the survivors consoled themselves by looking on themselves as first and foremost Americans. In the 1870s and 1880s the Irish became the majority population in New York. Even though they were poor, they wanted to succeed as Americans. Only when significant numbers of Irish had achieved this goal did they feel free to indulge in nostalgia for their country of origin.[4]

By the 1900s, second- and third-generation Irish Americans were established as a powerful part of the urban communities in which they had settled. Anti-Irish feeling had abated during the Civil War. Their involvement in politics, where again the strength of their numbers was an advantage, gave them an increasingly secure position in American society. Irish-American politicians made lavish efforts to secure better living conditions for their less fortunate countrymen, and by the early years of this century other groups of immigrants, such as Italians, Jews and Chinese, had replaced the Irish as objects of discrimination. By the early twentieth century the display of Irishness mounted on Saint Patrick's Day had become an important, and widely accepted part of Irish-American life. The Saint Patrick's Day parade provided an occasion where the community could celebrate not only its ethnic origin, but also its successful integration into American society.

It is largely because of the American example that Saint Patrick's Day is now celebrated the world over – Canada, Australia, Africa, South America and many European capitals all hold some kind of parade, big or small. Even cities where Irish connections are few, New Orleans or Puerto Rico, for example, hold highly successful parades: good-natured events which provide harmless fun – an excuse for communal merrymaking.

Things do not, at least from this side of the Atlantic look so innocuous as far as the Manhattan parade is concerned. The Ancient Order of Hibernians exerts rigid control over it. One of their 'inviolable rules' is that everyone marching has to be part of a group. When Robert F. Kennedy tried to join in the march spontaneously, he was 'escorted off Fifth Avenue and down a side street', according to the AOH's historian.[5] So was Brendan Behan, and, more recently, Jimmy Carter. He was at the time a presidential candidate, but the AOH proudly boasts of having made him stick to their rules.

Another rule governing the Manhattan parade states: 'No mottos, banners, signs or placards of any offensive or derogatory nature or of any commercial or advertising kind will be allowed There is a very important exception to this rule: banners with a political message – 'England get out of Ireland' – first approved and promoted as a marching slogan in 1948. More than 100 banners of this nature were carried in the 1980 parade. This offends and infuriates the Irish as much as, if not more than, it does the English. Such protests ignore the fact that the 'Irish problem' is not a British-versus-Irish struggle: it is a complex social and economic problem. It is neither helpful to the Irish, north and south, nor to Irish-American relations, to raise the issue in crude slogans on Saint Patrick's Day.

8
ALTHOUGH IT IS THE NIGHT

Armagh is a pleasant town, with several good Georgian buildings, but, owing to political unrest, daily life is carried on in a tense atmosphere of high security. It is, of course, the seat of the Catholic Archbishop of Ireland, having established its supremacy over other Irish dioceses by emphasizing its connections with Saint Patrick.

The proximity in Armagh of two cathedrals, one Protestant, one Catholic, both dedicated to the nation's patron saint, provides an excellent opportunity to examine the iconography which has grown up around the figure of Saint Patrick. He is enshrined in a stained-glass window in each cathedral. The Protestant cathedral is much older than the Catholic one – its shell dates from 1261 and, in a history typical of many Irish churches, it was destroyed in the sixteenth century, rebuilt in the seventeenth, burnt down again shortly after and remodelled several times between 1683 and 1802. The Catholic cathedral was begun in 1840, but work was abandoned during the famine and it was not completed until 1873.

The stained-glass windows of Saint Patrick in both cathedrals date from the late nineteenth century. The Catholic cathedral's Saint Patrick is the familiar patriarchal figure with flowing white hair and a long white beard, dressed in early seventeenth-century bishop's robes and carrying a jewelled crozier surmounted by a cross, with the serpents writhing at his feet beneath a few sprigs of shamrock.

The Protestant cathedral's Saint Patrick is not so instantly identifiable. He is a man of about thirty with short, dark hair and a neatly trimmed goatee beard. He is wearing a simple white tunic with a Roman-style cloak in purple and gold flung over one shoulder. In his left hand is a shepherd's crook. His feet, which are firmly planted on a bed of shamrock, are encased in elaborate Roman sandals. By an inexplicable oversight, the her- aldic shield over his head displays the Saint Andrew's cross – a white saltire on a blue ground – instead of Saint Patrick's red saltire. Few visitors, I was told, even the most distinguished ones, ever notice the blunder.

The Catholic church has remained faithful to an image of Saint Patrick which dates from the early seventeenth century: the earliest known example of this genre appeared as the frontis- piece to a collection of Irish saints' lives published in Paris in 1624. It has changed little since then. This version of Saint Pat- rick was widely disseminated when an almost identical bust of an elderly bearded Saint Patrick with a mitre and pastoral staff was used on the obverse of copper halfpenny coins issued in 1798.

Apart from the evidence of stone crosses, many of which are so weathered that it is hard to distinguish details, no pictorial rep- resentations of Saint Patrick survived the Reformation. Saint Patrick's staff, the *Baculus Jesu*, was publicly burnt by the Bishop of Dublin in 1538, and there are no records of what it looked like. The destruction of 'idolatrous images' in churches was carried out with great zeal for over twenty years. All knowledge of tradi- tional representation of Saint Patrick died out within a genera- tion, and the figure which appeared in 1624 represents the birth of an entirely new tradition.

The evidence of later twentieth-century representations of Saint Patrick in Ireland suggests that many artists – whether working in mosaic, paint, sculpture or stained glass – are choos- ing to represent Saint Patrick as a young Roman with a small beard or none at all. The Saint Patrick Heritage Centre in Downpatrick opts for a clean-shaven young Roman. The excep- tions to this rule are those works commissioned by the Catholic church. The statue at Tara is typical – a bearded and mitred bishop in flowing robes with a pastoral staff and his right hand raised in a blessing. There is a very similar statue erected at the base of Croaghpatrick, another on Station Island, in Granard, in Galway and numerous other Irish towns.

We can never know for certain what Saint Patrick looked like. Most people prefer, apparently, to see him as a bearded patriarch in seventeenth-century bishop's robes. It is monotonous and anachronistic, but also has a comforting predictability about it, part of the timeless consolation offered by religion. The young, beardless Roman makes a welcome change, but no one has yet managed to endow him with the *gravitas* of the more familiar patriarch.

It is difficult to establish exactly why and when the Church of Ireland opted for a young, Roman and often clean-shaven Saint Patrick, but it is most likely that this image originated during the latter part of the nineteenth century, when antiquarians were rediscovering the truth behind the legendary figure.

The lack of interest shown in Saint Patrick these days is all the more remarkable when contrasted with the fascination that he held for the Irish people up to the early 1960s. From the mid-nineteenth century there was an apparently insatiable appetite for books, pamphlets, newspaper articles and features about the patron saint. Some of this interest was inspired by religious devotion to the saint; some of it was nationalistic, the result of the identification of Saint Patrick with the nationalist cause. Some of it was sectarian and some of it was straightforward historical curiosity. In the mid-twentieth century every saloon-bar bore in Ireland could expound at length on the 'problem' of Saint Patrick: whether there was one Saint Patrick, two, or none at all.

The strangest feature of Patrician scholarship between the mid-nineteenth and mid-twentieth centuries was not so much the bizarreness of its ideas – odd though they were – but rather the passionate interest that the topic of the life and times of Saint Patrick aroused in the Irish public. Books which in retrospect seem highly abstruse and of limited appeal had a remarkably wide readership. Every new wave of academic *Lives* was the precursor of another wave, either giving a more accessible expression to the academics' insights, or strongly refuting them.

An odd feature of the legend of Saint Patrick in modern times is that its material has proved far more amenable to dissection and analysis by academics than it has to the attention it has received from the literati. Some of the worst verse that I have ever come across has been written in honour of our patron saint. With the exception of the special place that Lough Derg has acquired in the consciousness of modern Irish poets (notably Patrick Kavanagh, Denis Devlin and Seamus Heaney), most verse treatments, dramatizations and novelizations of Saint Patrick's life are dire stuff. Padraic Colum, playwright and poet, editor of *A Treasury of Irish Folklore* (1954), considers that the following ditty from Thomas Crofton Croker's *Popular Songs of Ireland* deserves to be ranked among 'the worst verse in the world':

> There's a dear little plant that grows in our isle,
> Twas Saint Patrick himself, sure, that set it;
> And the sun of his labour with pleasure did smile,
> And with dew from his eye often wet it.
> It thrives through the bog, through the brake, through the
>   mireland;
> And he called it the dear little Shamrock of Ireland.
>   The sweet little shamrock, the dear little shamrock,
>   The sweet little, green little, Shamrock of Ireland.

A much older and more fruitful poetic tradition links Saint Patrick with the warrior hero Finn, and his followers the Fianna, in tales referred to as the Fenian or Ossianic cycle. They are not associated with any particular historical era or place. Finn and his companions lived in a kind of Arcadia, hunting and feasting and occasionally going to war. *The Colloquy of the Old Men* (*Agallamh na Seanorach*) compiled in the twelfth century, tells of travels made around Ireland by two Fenian survivors, Caoilte mac Rónáin and Oisin, with Saint Patrick. At each resting-place they recall a heroic exploit of the past for the saint. These tales were made enormously popular by Aubrey de Vere, whose poems *The Legends of St Patrick* were first published in 1872, and reprinted many times. A devout Christian himself, de Vere manages to emphasize the attractions of Christianity without denigrating the paganism of the heroes of old. Patrick addresses Oisin:

'Old man, thou hearest our Christian hymns;
Such strains thou hadst never heard – '
'Thou liest, thou priest! for in Letter Lee wood
I have listened its famed blackbird!'

Yeats gives a far more complex treatment to the Fenian material in *The Wanderings of Oisin* (1889). Most of this long poem consists of Oisin's nostalgic memories of past events. Patrick's efforts to move the hero to repentance are futile; Oisin understands that the Fenians have been condemned to eternal hell-fire, but he insists that he would rather join them than 'gaze on the blessed and no man I loved of old there'.

Certain contemporary poets hold Saint Patrick in contempt because, by converting Ireland to Christianity, he brought an end to the romantic way of life of the Fenian heroes and replaced it with the narrow restrictions of Christianity. An extreme posture, and a somewhat fanciful one; nevertheless modern 'Fenians' see Saint Patrick as the worst thing that ever happened to Ireland: without him we would still be enjoying the glorious pagan pleasures of the heroes of old.

Efforts to make films and dramas out of the saint's life have not, so far, been successful. In 1961 the Irish Tourist Board sponsored in Dublin's Croke Park (venue for hurling and Gaelic football finals) a massive pageant based on the saint's life involving some 600 Dublin schoolchildren. The best moment in a dull and over-long production, according to several eye-witnesses, occurred during Patrick's battle with Loeghaire's Druids at Tara, when the pageant was suddenly disrupted by Brendan Behan and a crowd of friends roaring, 'UP THE DRUIDS!'

Patrician scholars, until quite recently, tended to disagree on just about everything. Their disagreements can usually be traced back to their definition of 'Patrician documents', that is to say, the sources that they rely on for evidence. The present-day tendency is to reject information found in everything except the *Confession* and *Letter to Coroticus*, unless it has impeccable corroboration from some other source. Until the early 1960s Muirchú and Tirechán were considered by some people to be reliable historians, if to be approached with caution. Many late nine-teenth- and early twentieth-century scholars laid great store by the 'facts' about Saint Patrick's mission that could be gleaned from the *Tripartite Life*. The less scientific among them (usually writers with a pious intent in the hagiographical spirit) insisted on the historical truth of Jocelin. In short, the scholars' conclusions depended largely on how much of which early *Lives* they were prepared to accept as historical truth.

Between 1864 and 1905, 26 serious full-length books on Saint Patrick were published, and 77 articles on him appeared in learned periodicals. In 1931 and 1932, when the first Patrician Year was celebrated, 16 books and 35 learned articles appeared. During 1961 and 1962, when the 1500th anniversary of Saint Patrick's death was being celebrated, a further 5 books and 37 articles of interest mainly to academics were published, as well as 13 books and 115 booklets and articles aimed at the general public.

'Saint Patrick', writes the novelist James Plunkett,[1] 'has always been a source of pride and complacency' to the Irish people – pride because he converted the nation so easily, and complacency because everyone thought that they knew who Saint Patrick was. When T. F. O'Rahilly proposed the existence of two Saint Patricks, the Irish people experienced little short of a collective national panic. Plunkett describes the mood in Dublin at that time:

> I can still recall the great scandal of 1942, when a book called *The Two Patricks* was published by a learned Irish Professor who advanced the theory that there was one Patrick (Palladius Patrick) whose mission lasted from 432–461, and another who arrived in 462 and died about 490. The suggestion caused a national unheaval. If the careers of the two Patricks, through scholarly bungling, had become inextricably entangled, who did what? And worse still – which of them was the patron saint? If you addressed a prayer to one, might it not be delivered by mistake to the other? There was a feeling abroad that any concession to the two Patricks theory would lead unfailingly to a theory of no Patrick at all.

O'Rahilly believed that the conversion of Ireland to Christianity was the work of two Patricks: the Palladius mentioned by Prosper of Aquitaine, sent to 'the Irish believing in Christ', and a later Patrick, author of the *Letter* and the *Confession*. The Saint Patrick of the Latin and Irish *Lives* is therefore a composite figure and his acts are the work of two different people.

O'Rahilly's theory was first delivered as a lecture at Dublin's new Institute of Advanced Studies, along with a paper by Professor Schroedinger of the Department of Cosmic Physics. The apparent absurdity of both the learned gentlemen's theses inspired the following item in the *Irish Times* 'Cruiskeen Lawn' column, written by Myles na Gopaleen (Flann O'Brien):

A friend has drawn my attention to Professor O'Rahilly's recent address on 'Palladius and Patrick'. I understand also that Professor Schroedinger has been proving lately that you cannot establish a first cause. The first fruit of the Institute therefore, has been an effort to show that there are two Saint Patricks and no God. The propagation of heresy and unbelief has nothing to do with polite learning, and unless we are careful this Institute of ours will make us the laughing stock of the world.

The two Patricks theory is by no means the oddest one. At one stage there were three Saint Patricks, then there were five; in 1902, Heinrich Zimmer, a German scholar, proved to his own satisfaction and that of many others that there had never been a Saint Patrick at all. Just how widespread this theory was in the early years of this century is indicated by the entry for Saint Patrick in the 1909 edition of the *Dictionary of National Biography*, supposedly a non-controversial standard work. Its final paragraph reads:

Notwithstanding the insurmountable difficulties which the apocryphal story of Saint Patrick involves, it was successfully palmed off on the Irish people by an active party in Ireland. This was rendered possible by the Danish tyranny and the exodus of learned men, for there was no one to criticize it until the

revival of learning in the twelfth century, and by then it was
too firmly established to be overthrown.

Another theory, which originated in the mid-nineteenth century and has its adherents to this day, is the assertion that Saint
Patrick had nothing to do with the Catholic church, but was
in fact the founder of the Episcopalian Church of Ireland. The
theory stands or falls on establishing whether or not Patrick
undertook his mission in Ireland with papal approval. If the
church he founded was not authorized by the Pope, then there
are ways (albeit somewhat tortuous) of arguing that the Church
of Ireland is the direct descendant of the church founded by Saint
Patrick. This point of view is explained at length in a highly
influential work by the Revd James Henthorn Todd DD,
published in 1864, *Saint Patrick, Apostle of Ireland*. Todd (1805–69)
was President of the Royal Irish Academy, and a senior Fellow of
Trinity College, Dublin, where he held the Chair of Regius Professor of Hebrew and later distinguished himself as Librarian.
His obituary says that he 'was one of the best known Irishmen
of his day, consulted both by statesmen and theologians'. This is
hardly a person to dismiss as a crackpot.

From the earliest days of modern Patrician studies, Saint
Patrick's biographers can be divided into two distinct groups:
'rational' scholars who attempt to distinguish between legend
and historical fact, and the so-called 'pre-critical' school who are
determined to hang on to as much as possible of the traditional Saint Patrick (exemplified by Jocelin's *Life*): the renowned
miracle-worker who converted Ireland single-handedly without
a drop of blood being shed.

As knowledge advanced and became increasingly institutionalized in the twentieth century, those pre-critical *Lives* of
Saint Patrick still being written are mostly the work of religious
propagandists outside the world of academia. Among the academics the debate becomes involved with minutiae: details of
chronology, the location of Patrick's education and birthplace,
the question of who sent him on his Irish mission, the extent of
that mission, and the admissibility or not of evidence from the
Irish Annals and the *Book of Armagh*. There is much quibbling

over the precise interpretation of certain supposedly crucial passages in the *Confession*.

By the early 1960s the whole business had become so convoluted and specialized that the majority of books and learned articles on Saint Patrick ceased to hold any attraction for the general reader. There is a marked decline in the number of academic books and papers published on Patrician topics after the early 1960s, and by the 1980s Patrician studies had become a highly specialized field. Its debates are characterized nowadays by a welcome enthusiasm for the writings of the historical Patricius. The current generation of Patrician scholars believes that earlier generations, while producing much valuable work, tended to complicate matters unnecessarily by seeing problems where none in fact exist. Instead of reading the *Confession* as an elaborate riddle, the attitude today is to take its statements at face value as the pronouncements of a historical early Irish bishop of remarkable spiritual stature – that is to say, Saint Patrick. In fact, the history of Patrician studies can be described as the process of gradual rejection of all legendary material associated with the saint until we are left with the historical figure who wrote the *Confession* and the *Letter to Coroticus* and about whom, it is at last admitted, we actually know very little. In 1983, R. P. C. Hanson summed up the current state of knowledge about the historical Saint Patrick:[2]

The conventional picture of Saint Patrick presents him as a modern bishop with mitre and pastoral staff, banishing snakes from Ireland, teaching the doctrine of the Trinity by the example of the shamrock, overcoming the opposition of the High-King of Ireland, holding familiar concourse with a guardian angel, climbing Croagh Patrick in Co. Mayo to commune with God on the top, revisiting Mount Slemish in Co. Antrim where he is supposed to have spent an earlier period of captivity. It has represented him as a product of a Gaelic education in Auxerre or Lérins, the legate of a papal mission.

Not a single one of these details is historical: mitres were not invented for at least 500 years after Patrick's day. The story of his banishing snakes was concocted about three hundred years after his death, that of his teaching by means of the shamrock about a thousand years after his time. There was no High-King of Ireland in his day; the colourful story of his encounter with King Loeghaire at Tara is sheer fiction. He spent a captivity in Ireland indeed, but not on Mount Slemish. The Angel Victor is the confused corruption of the name of a man whom he once mentions as having seen in a dream. He did not climb Croagh Patrick, he was not educated in Gaul, he was not sent to Ireland by the bishop of Rome. All the exciting and glamorous features that tradition has attached to Patrick must be removed if we wish to know what he was really like. And yet the historical Saint Patrick is more interesting and more worth studying than all these later gaudy traditions.

The massive labours undertaken by Patrician scholars in the nineteenth century had two very important side-effects. Patrician studies made a significant contribution to historical knowledge of early Ireland, and also provided a major stimulus for a revival of scholarly interest in the Irish language.

Knowledge of pagan Ireland was slow to emerge in the nineteenth century. People were wary of the new revelations being made, and it was many years before the truth about the 'godless' nature of early Irish society became common knowledge. The desire to know more about the life of Saint Patrick and his successors provided an impeccably respectable motive for investigating the real and possibly unsavoury nature of pre-Christian Irish society, and removing the veil of ignorance which covered the practices of its 'uncouth' kings and druids and warriors. The antiquarians' *Lives* of Saint Patrick revealed a far more complex and historically truthful picture of pre-Christian Ireland than the popular version peddled by the balladmongers, and those who read their books were intrigued. That was, initially, an important part of the wide appeal of biographies of Saint Patrick.

In order to produce original research into Saint Patrick, at a time when the *Tripartite Life* was still considered an important source of information, it was necessary for scholars to have a good knowledge of written Irish. James Henthorn Todd, whose influential book, claiming Saint Patrick as the founder of the

Episcopalian church was first published in 1864, was one of the first scholars to master written Irish.

At that time the Irish language was in a bad state of neglect. English-language National Schools had been established throughout the country since 1831. English was the language of politics, law, commerce and education, and anyone who wished to advance themselves had to speak English. Many people still spoke Irish at home, and many of the landlord class – Daniel O'Connell (The Liberator), for example – could converse in Irish with their tenants. But it was not until Todd's generation of antiquarians began their researches that the Irish intelligentsia started to realize the importance of a knowledge of the Irish language for gaining a knowledge of the past. The majority of readers in 1864 would find Irish proper names just as 'uncouth' as Jocelin did in 1185.

Todd's book naturally caused outrage among the Catholic community. He argued that contemporary Irish Catholicism had nothing at all to do with Saint Patrick's conversion of Ireland, but was a foreign import, the original Irish Catholic church having died out during the period between the Viking invasions and the Reformation. Catholics wanted to refute Todd's assertions, but were unable to produce from their midst a scholar of Todd's stature with the necessary knowledge of Irish to carry out the task.

In 1843, Todd was one of the founders of Saint Columba's College, Rathfarnham, which, besides providing a classical education, was also a place where those intending to take orders in the Church of Ireland could be taught Irish – a major innovation.

Catholic seminarians had no such encouragement to pursue their study of the Irish language. At Maynooth, the largest seminary in the British Isles, the study of Irish was badly neglected throughout the nineteenth century. In 1890, Father O'Growney, one of the co-founders of the Gaelic League, wrote a strongly-worded article deploring the lack of interest shown by Irish Catholics in their native language and its literature. He presented the matter of the controversy over Saint Patrick's heritage as a major reason why Irish Catholics should learn to read and write their own language:

Upon us Irish Catholics the study of Irish literature has a special claim. We maintain that the faith we hold is identical with that taught by Saint Patrick and his successors; that they were, as we are, Roman Catholics. It has been the aim of Protestant Irishmen to persuade their co-religionists that they alone hold the pure Patrician teaching, now, as always, uninfluenced by Rome. Strong articles by good writers have appeared quite recently in support of their contention, and very probably this historico-religious question will be discussed warmly in a short time . . . If this discussion were put upon us tomorrow how many have we competent to support our claim by arguments drawn from our extensive ecclesiastical literature? . . . It has been shown that those who study the literature are practically non-Catholics, and such men might not see, or might be tempted to slur over a point in favour of our position.

Saint Patrick is given credit for all sorts of wonderful deeds, but seldom is the important role that he played in the revival of the Irish language among the academic community given the prominence due to it.

As it happened, the next wave of distinguished Patrician scholars did not emerge from Maynooth, but from University College, Dublin – the successor to the Catholic University set up by Cardinal Newman. Prominent among them was Eóin Mac Neill (1867–1945), co-founder of the Gaelic League. He was famous both as a patriot – he was Chief of Staff of the Irish Volunteers in 1916 – and as a scholar. His *Life* of Saint Patrick (1934) can still be found on the shelves of most Irish public libraries.

The heated scholarly debate about Saint Patrick reached a grand climax, which in retrospect was also a kind of finale, in 1961, which was declared a Patrician year by the Catholic hierarchy to commemorate the anniversary of Saint Patrick's death in 461. His arrival in 432 had already been celebrated in 1932, and resulted in the building of separate Catholic and Church of Ireland monuments at Saul.

The souvenir brochures of the 1961 celebrations remind us forcibly of what a drab, priest-ridden country Ireland was at that time, before the advent of the economic boom and Vatican II. Dutiful crowds in long overcoats huddle under umbrellas outside Armagh Cathedral to watch President de Valera arrive for the official ceremonies, from which most of the lay onlookers will be excluded. A procession of priests advances through the drizzle, their vestments flapping in the wind, followed by a similarly windswept procession of prelates and abbots, a procession of bishops and archbishops, a procession of cardinals, and finally the papal legate and his suite. The seven archbishops present, photographed together in their various fancy mitres, look more comical than imposing.

The 1961 Patrician year had a dual purpose. Besides celebrating the 1500th anniversary of Saint Patrick's death, it was also a celebration of the Irish missionary movement 'in which Saint Patrick's spirit lives on'. For the general public, the exhibition of the work of Irish missionaries mounted for the occasion held far more interest than the pomp and ceremony of the hierarchy.

The Irish people have always had a unique enthusiasm for foreign missions, and the church in Ireland has made much use of the figure of Saint Patrick as a prototype missionary. The argument ran that Saint Patrick sacrificed everything to come to pagan Ireland as a missionary, and convert her people to Christianity. Therefore, in gratitude for the gift of faith that he bestowed upon them, the Irish people had a special duty to take that gift of faith abroad and bestow it on the 'pagan' African or Chinese or South Americans that they found there. Irish missionaries today view their work in a rather different light, but they still acknowledge the importance of the inspiration of the figure of Saint Patrick.

In modern times the Irish have made a disproportionately large contribution, both in manpower and finance, to the development of overseas missions. The most striking example of how deeply entrenched this tradition is in Ireland was in the donation made by the Irish people to Live Aid in 1985: over £7 million was raised from a population of only 3½ million people. Live Aid was the brainchild of Bob Geldof, an Irishman educated in

Dublin during the 1960s, when missionary appeals were a regular feature of the Irish primary school classroom.

The missionary movement was numerically at its peak in the 1960s. In 1960, 1240 men and women left Ireland for, as they were called in those days, 'pagan mission fields'. In 1961 there were over 1000 Irish priests and almost 2000 Irish nuns in Africa alone. (These figures include only Irish-born missionaries originating in Ireland, not those of Irish descent.) In 1968 the total of Irish priests, nuns and laity working in African missions was an impressive 4473. Another 2027 Irish missionaries were working in Asia, and there were 585 in Central and South America.

The great pride taken by the Irish people in the strength of their overseas missionary movement is evident in the 1961 publications, even though it is expressed in a terminology which seems archaic today, abounding in references to 'pagans' and their 'heathenism'. Things have changed a great deal since those days. There is some concern over a decline in the number of vocations to the priesthood, but the most recently available statistics for Irish missionaries abroad (1981) show only a slight decline on those for 1968.

By 1981 the emphasis on 'converting heathens' had entirely disappeared, and the Irish Missionary Union could claim that of approximately '6000 Irish missionary workers in Africa, Asia and Latin America, 3725 are engaged full-time in works of development such as education, health, medicine, communications, agricultural projects and other social activities. This is possibly the greatest per capita contribution of any developed country to the socio-economic development of the Third World.'

During the years since the celebration of the Patrician Year of 1961, Ireland has undergone many changes. In Northern Ireland sectarian violence has, since the late 1960s, disrupted normal life. Entry into the European Economic Community (1973) has done much to produce a more cosmopolitan, less insular society in the Republic. However, the economic boom of the 1970s quickly turned into an economic slump in the 1980s, with widespread unemployment. Emigration, notably the exodus of young graduates, is once again a matter for concern. Ireland has the youngest population in the EEC, with one-third of it concentrated in the Dublin area. National television broadcasting was only introduced in the early 1960s; nowadays most of the population has a multichannel choice of viewing: they watch *Dallas* on the Aran Islands. There is talk of the Catholic Church losing its traditionally strong hold on the people: yet the Pope's visit in 1979 was a triumphant success, especially with the youth of the country, and in 1986 over two-thirds of those who voted in the referendum on divorce were against its legalization.

Not surprisingly, in view of the dramatic changes in living standards and the increased emphasis on material prosperity during the boom years, the past quarter of a century has witnessed a noticeable decline of interest in the Saint Patrick legend among certain sectors of the community, particularly urban sophisticates. A major new characteristic of the cult of Saint Patrick in late twentieth-century Ireland is the disappearance of the figure of Saint Patrick that, up until relatively recent times, was an important character in Irish folklore tradition.

I, for one, am not sorry to see him go. Innumerable Saint Patrick stories current in oral tradition up until the 1930s appear in print these days mainly in handbooks of Irish legend and folklore aimed at the tourist market. They belong to another age. They are simple folk-tales, many of them probably of medieval origin. They were cherished by the rural Irish-speaking community. Some of them derive from the *Tripartite Life*, and some from Muirchú, but by no means all of them do. The Saint Patrick featured in them is often bad-tempered and has the powers of a wizard rather than a Christian saint. The most remarkable quality of these folk-tales is the affection and familiarity with which Saint Patrick is regarded. He is an informal fellow, very inclined to drop in on people for a chat, in the course of which he identifies and solves their problems. In some legends he is made responsible for otherwise inexplicable quirks of nature: the salmon has the power to jump because a salmon once leapt into Saint Patrick's lap when he was hungry, and he blessed it with the gift of jumping; the tips of the rushes are black because when Saint Patrick cursed Ireland in his sleep his companion deflected the curse on to the rushes.

Saint Patrick invented cats and dogs when he dropped in for a chat with a good man who had, unknowingly, married the devil's mother. They had two children, a boy and a girl. The saint banished the woman from her home in a ball of fire, but he took pity on the children and changed the boy into a dog and the girl into a cat, and this is why those two animals have something of human nature in them.

And so on. There are many such legends. Taken in combination with the number of holy wells, sacred stones, rivers, churches, mountains, roads, and prints of hands, feet and knees left in rocks, all allegedly associated with the saint, it is no wonder that many tourists find their eyes glazing over at the very mention of his name, and that his countrymen find it all something of an embarrassment.

Many of the smaller pilgrimages traditionally associated with Saint Patrick are dying out. The stations traditionally observed before and after climbing the Reek, for example, in the village of Aghagower were still observed in the late 1950s: now they are only a vague memory for a few old people. I have come across numerous wells and stones associated with Saint Patrick in a bad state of neglect, their whereabouts known only to members of the local historical societies. As long as their location and history are recorded by such dedicated organizations, I see no need to regret the disappearance of such observances, based, as they were, on specious tradition and superstition.

Sites with a more substantial claim to authenticity, and a greater appeal to the imagination, continue to be popular. Croaghpatrick and Lough Derg attract thousands of pilgrims every year. It is hard to say how many people nowadays take Croaghpatrick seriously as a penance: not a great number, I suspect. Most people find the climb an enjoyable and exhilarating experience with an interesting history behind it. For the physically fit and well-shod, the Croaghpatrick pilgrimage is a great outing.

Lough Derg, in contrast, is not a pilgrimage to be undertaken lightly. It bears witness to a remarkable survival of the religion that was brought to Ireland in the fifth century by the young Romano-British bishop whom we know as Saint Patrick. Lough Derg only survives because the people want it to. As long as there are people in Ireland prepared to go as pilgrims to Lough Derg, Ireland can never be accused of a lack of reverence for its patron saint.

It is at Lough Derg that Saint Patrick's spirituality can be found. It is a unique place, a place apart from modern Ireland, yet central to its core. This is where the search for Saint Patrick must end:

> How well I know that fountain, filling, running,
>   although it is the night.
>
> That eternal fountain, hidden away,
> I know its haven and its secrecy
>   although it is the night.
>
> But not its source because it does not have one,
> which is all sources' source and origin
>   although it is the night.
>
> No other thing can be so beautiful.
> Here the earth and heaven drink their fill
>   although it is the night.
>
> So pellucid it can never be muddied,
> and I know that all light radiates from it
>   although it is the night.
>
> I know no sounding line can find its bottom,
> nobody ford or plumb its deepest fathom
>   although it is the night.
>
> And its current so in flood it overspills
> to water hell and heaven and all peoples
>   although it is the night.
>
> And the current that is generated there,
> as far as it wills to, it can flow that far
>   although it is the night.

And from these two a third current proceeds
which neither of these two, I know, precedes
  although it is the night.

This eternal fountain hides and splashes
within this living bread that is life to us
  although it is the night.

Hear it calling out to every creature.
And they drink these waters, although it is dark here
  because it is the night.

I am repining for this living fountain.
With this bread of life I see it plain
  although it is the night.[3]

APPENDIX I
The Writings of Saint Patrick

CONFESSION

I am Patrick, a sinner, most unlearned, the least of all the faithful, and utterly despised by many. My father was Calpornius, a deacon, son of Potitus, a priest, of the village Bannavem Taburniae; he had a country seat nearby, and there I was taken captive.

I was then about sixteen years of age. I did not know the true God. I was taken into captivity to Ireland with many thousands of people – and deservedly so, because we turned away from God, and did not keep His commandments, and did not obey our priests, who used to remind us of our salvation. And the Lord brought over us the wrath of His anger and scatte.ed us among many nations, even unto the utmost part of the earth, where now my littleness is placed among strangers.

And there the Lord opened the sense of my unbelief that I might at last remember my sins and be converted with all my heart to the Lord my God, who had regard for my abjection, and mercy on my youth and ignorance, and watched over me before I knew Him, and before I was able to distinguish between good and evil, and guarded me, and comforted me as would a father his son.

Hence I cannot be silent – nor, indeed, is it expedient – about the great benefits and the great grace which the Lord has deigned to bestow upon me in the land of my captivity; for this we can give to God in return after having been chastened by Him, to exalt and praise His wonders before every nation that is anywhere under the heaven.

Because there is no other God, nor ever was, nor will be, than God the Father unbegotten, without beginning, from whom is all beginning, the Lord of the universe, as we have been taught; and His son Jesus Christ, whom we declare to have always been with the Father, spiritually and ineffably begotten by the Father before the beginning of the world, before all beginning; and by Him are made all things visible and invisible. He was made man, and, having defeated death, was received into heaven by the Father; and He hath given Him all power over all names in heaven, on earth, and under the earth, and every tongue shall confess to Him that Jesus Christ is Lord and God, in whom we believe, and whose advent we expect soon to be, judge of the living and of the dead, who will render to every man according to his deeds; and He has poured forth upon us abundantly the Holy Spirit, the gift and pledge of immortality, who makes those who believe and obey sons of God and joint heirs with Christ; and Him do we confess and adore, one God in the Trinity of the Holy Name.

For He Himself has said through the Prophet: Call upon me in the day of thy trouble, and I will deliver thee, and thou shalt glorify me. And again He says: It is honourable to reveal and confess the works of God.

Although I am imperfect in many things, I nevertheless wish that my brethren and kinsmen should know what sort of person I am, so that they may understand my heart's desire.

I know well the testimony of my Lord, who in the Psalm declares: Thou wilt destroy them that speak a lie. And again He says: The mouth that belieth killeth the soul. And the same Lord says in the Gospel: Every idle word that men shall speak, they shall render an account for it on the day of judgement.

And so I should dread exceedingly, with fear and trembling, this sentence on that day when no one will be able to escape or hide, but we all, without exception, shall have to give an account even of our smallest sins before the judgement of the Lord Christ.

For this reason I had in mind to write, but hesitated until now; I was afraid of exposing myself to the talk of men, because I have not studied like the others, who thoroughly imbibed law and Sacred Scripture, and never had to change from the language of their childhood days, but were able to make it still more perfect. In our case, what I had to say had to be translated into a tongue foreign to me, as can be easily proved from the savour of my writing, which betrays how little instruction and training I have had in the art of words; for, so says Scripture, by the tongue will be discovered the wise man, and understanding, and knowledge, and the teaching of truth.

But of what help is an excuse, however true, especially if combined with presumption, since now, in my old age, I strive for something that I did not acquire in youth? It was my sins that prevented me from fixing in my mind what before I had barely read through. But who believes me, though I should repeat what I started out with?

As a youth, nay, almost as a boy not able to speak, I was taken captive, before I knew what to pursue and what to avoid. Hence to-day I blush and fear exceedingly to reveal my lack of education; for I am unable to tell my story to those versed in the art of concise writing – in such a way, I mean, as my spirit and mind long to do, and so that the sense of my words expresses what I feel.

But if indeed it had been given to me as it was given to others, then I would not be silent because of my desire of thanksgiving; and if perhaps some people think me arrogant for doing so in spite of my lack of knowledge and my slow tongue, it is, after all, written: The stammering tongues shall quickly learn to speak peace.

How much more should we earnestly strive to do this, we, who are, so Scripture says, a letter of Christ for salvation unto the utmost part of the earth, and, though not an eloquent one, yet . . . written in your hearts, not with ink, but with the spirit of the living God! And again the Spirit witnesses that even rusticity was created by the Highest.

Whence I, once rustic, exiled, unlearned, who does not know how to provide for the future, this at least I know most certainly that before I was humiliated I was like a stone lying in the deep mire; and He that is mighty came and in His mercy lifted me up, and raised me aloft, and placed me on the top of the wall. And therefore I ought to cry out aloud and so also render something to the Lord for His great benefits here and in eternity – benefits which the mind of men is unable to appraise.

Wherefore, then, be astonished, ye great and little that fear God, and you men of letters on your estates, listen and pore over this. Who was it that roused up me, the fool that I am, from the midst of those who in the eyes of men are wise, and expert in law, and powerful in word and in everything? And He inspired me – me, the outcast of this world – before others, to be the man (if only I could!) who, with fear and reverence and without blame, should faithfully serve the people to whom the love of Christ conveyed and gave me for the duration of my life, if I should be worthy; yes indeed, to serve them humbly and sincerely.

In the light, therefore, of our faith in the Trinity I must make this choice, regardless of danger I must make known the gift of God and everlasting consolation, without fear and frankly I must spread everywhere the name of God so that after my decease I may leave a bequest to my brethren and sons whom I have baptised in the Lord – so many thousands of people.

And I was not worthy, nor was I such that the Lord should grant this to His servant; that after my misfortunes and so great difficulties, after my captivity, after the lapse of so many years, He should give me so great a grace in behalf of that nation – a thing which once, in my youth, I never expected nor thought of.

But after I came to Ireland – every day I had to tend sheep, and many times a day I prayed – the love of God and His fear came to me more and more, and my faith was strengthened. And my spirit was moved so that in a single day I would say as many as a hundred prayers, and almost as many in the night, and this even when I was staying in the woods and on the mountains; and I used to get up for prayer before daylight, through snow, through frost, through rain, and I felt no harm, and there was no sloth in me – as I now see, because the spirit within me was then fervent.

And there one night I heard in my sleep a voice saying to me: 'It is well that you fast, soon you will go to your own country.' And again, after a short while, I heard a voice saying to me: 'See, your ship is ready.' And it was not near, but at a distance of perhaps two hundred miles, and I had never been there, nor did I know a living soul there; and then I took to flight, and I left the man with whom I had stayed for six years. And I went in the strength of God who directed my way to my good, and I feared nothing until I came to that ship.

And the day that I arrived the ship was set afloat, and I said that I was able to pay for my passage with them. But the captain was not pleased, and with indignation he answered harshly: 'It is of no use for you to ask us to go along with us.' And when I heard this, I left them in order to return to the hut where I was staying. And as I went, I began to pray; and before I had ended my prayer, I heard one of them shouting behind me, 'Come, hurry, we shall take you on in good faith; make friends with us in whatever way you like.' And so on that day I refused to suck their breasts for fear of God, but rather hoped they would come to the faith of Jesus Christ, because they were pagans. And thus I had my way with them, and we set sail at once.

And after three days we reached land, and for twenty-eight days we travelled through deserted country. And they lacked food, and hunger overcame them; and the next day the captain said to me: 'Tell me, Christian: you say that your God is great and all-powerful; why, then, do you not pray for us? As you can see, we are suffering from hunger; it is unlikely indeed that we shall ever see a human being again.'

I said to them full of confidence: 'Be truly converted with all your heart to the Lord my God, because nothing is impossible for Him, that this day He may send you food on your way until you be satisfied; for He has abundance everywhere.' And, with the help of God, so it came to pass: suddenly a herd of pigs appeared on the road before our eyes, and they killed many of them; and there they stopped for two nights and fully recovered their strength, and their hounds received their fill, for many of them had grown weak and were half-dead along the way. And from that day they had plenty of food. They also found wild honey, and offered some of it to me, and one of them said: 'This we offer in sacrifice.' Thanks be to God, I tasted none of it.

That same night, when I was asleep, Satan assailed me violently, a thing I shall remember as long as I shall be in this body. And he fell upon me like a huge rock, and I could not stir a limb. But whence came it into my mind, ignorant as I am, to call upon Helias? And meanwhile I saw the sun rise in the sky, and while I was shouting 'Helias! Helias' with all my might, suddenly the splendour of that sun fell on me and immediately freed me of all misery. And I believe that I was sustained by Christ my Lord, and that His Spirit was even then crying out in my behalf, and I hope it will be so on the day of my tribulation, as is written in the Gospel: On that day, the Lord declares, it is not you that speak, but the Spirit of your Father that speaketh in you.

And once again, after many years, I fell into captivity. On that first night I stayed with them. I heard a divine message saying to me: 'Two months will you be with them.' And so it came to pass: on the sixtieth night thereafter the Lord delivered me out of their hands.

Also on our way God gave us food and fire and dry weather every day, until, on the tenth day, we met people. As I said above, we travelled twenty-eight days through deserted country, and the night that we met people we had no food left.

And again after a few years I was in Britain with my people, who received me as their son, and sincerely besought me that now at last, having suffered so many hardships, I should not leave them and go elsewhere.

And there I saw in the night the vision of a man, whose name was Victoricus, coming as it were from Ireland, with countless letters. And he gave me one of them, and I read the opening words of the letter, which were, 'The voice of the Irish'; and as I read the beginning of the letter I thought that at the same moment I heard their voice – they were those beside the Wood of Voclut, which is near the Western Sea – and thus did they cry out as with one mouth: 'We ask thee, boy, come and walk among us once more.'

And I was quite broken in heart, and could read no further, and so I woke up. Thanks be to God, after many years the Lord gave to them according to their cry.

And another night – whether within me, or beside me, I know not, God knoweth – they called me most unmistakably with words which I heard but could not understand, except that at the end of the prayer He spoke thus: 'He that has laid down His life for thee, it is He that speaketh in thee'; and so I awoke full of joy.

And again I saw Him praying in me, and I was as it were within my body, and I heard Him above me, that is, over the inward man, and there He prayed mightily with groanings. And all the time I was astonished, and wondered, and thought with myself who it could be that prayed in me. But at the end of the prayer He spoke, saying that He was the Spirit; and so I woke up, and remembered the Apostle saying: The Spirit helpeth the infirmities of our prayer. For we know not what we should pray for as we ought; but the Spirit Himself asketh for us with unspeakable groanings, which cannot be expressed in words; and again: The Lord our advocate asketh for us.

And when I was attacked by a number of my seniors who came forth and brought up my sins against my laborious episcopate, on that day indeed was I struck so that I might have fallen now and for eternity; but the Lord graciously spared the stranger and sojourner for His name and came mightily to my help in this affliction. Verily, not slight was the shame and blame that fell upon me! I ask God that it may not be reckoned to them as sin.

As cause for proceeding against me they found – after thirty years! – a confession I had made before I was a deacon. In the anxiety of my troubled mind I confided to my dearest friend what I had done in my boyhood one day, nay, in one hour, because I was not yet strong. I know not, God knoweth – whether I was then fifteen years old; and I did not believe in the living God, nor did I so from my childhood, but lived in death and unbelief until I was severely chastised and really humiliated, by hunger and nakedness, and that daily.

On the other hand, I did not go to Ireland of my own accord, not until I had nearly perished; but this was rather for my good, for thus was I purged by the Lord; and He made me fit so that I might be now what was once far from me – that I should care and labour for the salvation of others, whereas then I did not even care about myself.

On that day, then, when I was rejected by those referred to and mentioned above, in that night I saw a vision of the night. There was a writing without honour against my face, and at the same time I heard God's voice saying to me: 'We have seen with displeasure the face of Deisignatus' (thus revealing his name). He did not say, 'Thou hast seen,' but 'We have seen,' as if He included Himself, as He sayeth: He who toucheth you toucheth as it were the apple of my eye.

Therefore I give Him thanks who hath strengthened me in everything, as He did not frustrate the journey upon which I had decided, and the work which I had learned from Christ my Lord; but I rather felt after this no little strength, and my trust was proved right before God and men.

And so I say boldly, my conscience does not blame me now or in the future:

God is my witness that I have not lied in the account which I have given you.

But the more am I sorry for my dearest friend that we had to hear what he said. To him I had confided my very soul! And I was told by some of the brethren before that defence – at which I was not present, nor was I in Britain, nor was it suggested by me – that he would stand up for me in my absence. He had even said to me in person: 'Look, you should be raised to the rank of bishop!' – of which I was not worthy. But whence did it come to him afterwards that he let me down before all, good and evil, and publicly, in a matter in which he had favoured me before spontaneously and gladly – and not he alone, but the Lord, who is greater than all?

Enough of this. I must not, however, hide God's gift which He bestowed upon me in the land of my captivity; because then I earnestly sought Him, and there I found Him, and He saved me from all evil because – so I believe – of His Spirit that dwelleth in me. Again, boldly said. But God knows it, had this been said to me by a man, I had perhaps remained silent for the love of Christ.

Hence, then, I give unwearied thanks to God, who kept me faithful in the day of my temptation, so that today I can confidently offer Him my soul as a living sacrifice – to Christ my Lord, who saved me out of all my troubles. Thus I can say: 'Who am I, O Lord, and to what hast Thou called me, Thou who didst assist me with such divine power that to-day I constantly exalt and magnify Thy name among the heathens wherever I may be, and not only in good days but also in tribulations? So indeed I must accept with equanimity whatever befalls me, be it good or evil, and always give thanks to God, who taught me to trust in Him always without hesitation, and who must have heard my prayer so that I, however ignorant I was, in the last days dared to undertake such a holy and wonderful work – thus imitating somehow those who, as the Lord once foretold, would preach His Gospel for a testimony to all nations before the end of the world. So we have seen it, and so it has been fulfilled: indeed, we are witnesses that the Gospel has been preached unto those parts beyond which there lives nobody.

Now, it would be tedious to give a detailed account of all my labours or even a part of them. Let me tell you briefly how the merciful God often freed me from slavery and from twelve dangers in which my life was at stake – not to mention numerous plots, which I cannot express in words; for I do not want to bore my readers. But God is my witness, who knows all things even before they come to pass, as He used to forewarn even me, poor wretch that I am, of many things by a divine message.

How came I by this wisdom, which was not in me, who neither knew the number of my days nor knew what God was? Whence was given to me afterwards the gift so great, so salutary – to know God and to love Him, although at the price of leaving my country and my parents?

And many gifts were offered to me in sorrow and tears, and I offended the donors, much against the wishes of some of my seniors; but, guided by God, in no way did I agree with them or acquiesce. It was not grace of my own, but God, who is strong in me and resists them all – as He had done when I came to the people of Ireland to preach the Gospel, and to suffer insult from the unbelievers, hearing the reproach of my going abroad, and many persecutions even unto bonds, and to give my free birth for the benefit of others; and, should I be worthy, I am prepared to give even my life without hesitation and most gladly for His name, and it is there that I wish to spend it until I die, if the Lord would grant it to me.

For I am very much God's debtor, who gave me such grace that many people were reborn in God through me and afterwards confirmed, and that clerics were ordained for them everywhere, for a people just coming to the faith, whom the Lord took from the utmost parts of the earth, as He once had promised through His prophets: To Thee the gentiles shall come from the ends of the earth and shall say: 'How false are the idols that our fathers got for themselves, and there is no profit in them'; and again: I have set Thee as a light among the gentiles, that Thou mayest be for salvation unto the utmost part of the earth.

And there I wish to wait for His promise who surely never deceives, as He promises in the Gospel: They shall come from the east and the west, and shall sit down with Abraham and Isaac and Jacob – as we believe the faithful will come from all the world.

For that reason, therefore, we ought to fish well and diligently, as the Lord exhorts in advance and teaches, saying: Come ye after me, and I will make you to be fishers of men. And again He says through the prophets: Behold, I send many fishers and hunters, saith God, and so on. Hence it was most necessary to spread our nets so that a great multitude and throng might be caught for God, and that there be clerics everywhere to baptize and exhort a people in need and want, as the Lord in the Gospel states, exhorts and teaches, saying: Going therefore now, teach ye all nations, baptizing them in the name of the Father, and the Son, and the Holy Spirit, teaching them to observe all things whatsoever I have commanded you: and behold I am with you all days even to the consummation of the world. And again He says: Go ye therefore into the whole world, and preach the Gospel to every creature. He that believeth and is baptized shall be saved; but he that believeth not shall be condemned. And again: This Gospel of the kingdom shall be preached in the whole world for a testimony to all nations, and then shall come the end. And so too the Lord announces through the prophet, and says: And it shall come to pass, in the last days, saith the Lord, I will pour out of my Spirit upon all flesh; and your sons and your daughters shall prophesy, and your young men shall see visions, and your old men shall dream dreams. And upon my servants indeed, and upon my handmaids will I pour out in those days of my Spirit, and they shall prophesy. And in *Osee* He saith: 'I will call that which was not my people, my people; . . . and her that had not obtained mercy, one that hath obtained mercy. And it shall be in the place where it was said: "You are not my people," there they shall be called the sons of the living God.'

Hence, how did it come to pass in Ireland that those who never had a knowledge of God, but until now always worshipped idols and things impure, have now been made a people of the Lord, and are called sons of God, that the sons and daughters of the kings of the Irish are seen to be monks and virgins of Christ?

Among others, a blessed Irishwoman of noble birth, beautiful, full-grown, whom I had baptized, came to us after some days for a particular reason: she told us that she had received a message from a messenger of God, and he admonished her to be a virgin of Christ and draw near to God. Thanks be to God, on the sixth day after this she most laudably and eagerly chose what all virgins of Christ do. Not that their fathers agree with them; no – they often ever suffer persecution and undeserved reproaches from their parents; and yet their number is ever increasing. How many have been reborn there so as to be of our kind, I do not know – not to mention widows and those who practise continence.

But greatest is the suffering of those women who live in slavery. All the time they have to endure terror and threats. But the Lord gave His grace to many of His maidens; for, though they are forbidden to do so, they follow Him bravely.

Wherefore, then, even if I wished to leave them and go to Britain – and how I would have loved to go to my country and my parents, and also to Gaul in order to visit the brethren and to see the face of the saints of my Lord! God knows it that I much desired it; but I am bound by the Spirit, who gives evidence against me if I do this, telling me that I shall be guilty; and I am afraid of losing the labour which I have begun – nay, not I, but Christ the Lord who bade me come here and stay with them for the rest of my life, if the Lord will, and will guard me from every evil way that I may not sin before Him.

This, I presume, I ought to do, but I do not trust myself as long as I am in this body of death, for strong is he who daily strives to turn me away from the faith and the purity of true religion to which I have devoted myself to the end of my life to Christ my Lord. But the hostile flesh is ever dragging us unto death, that is, towards the forbidden satisfaction of one's desires; and I know that in part I did not lead a perfect life as did the other faithful; but I acknowledge it to my Lord, and do not blush before Him, because I lie not: from the time I came to know Him in my youth, the love of God and the fear of Him have grown in me, and up to now, thanks to the grace of God, I have kept the faith.

And let those who will, laugh and scorn – I shall not be silent; nor shall I hide the signs and wonders which the Lord has shown me many years before they came to pass, as He knows everything even before the times of the world.

Hence I ought unceasingly to give thanks to God who often pardoned my folly and my carelessness, and on more than one occasion spared His great wrath on me, who was chosen to be His helper and who was slow to do as was shown me and as the Spirit suggested. And the Lord had mercy on me thousands and thousands of times because He saw that I was ready, but that I did not know what to do in the circumstances. For many tried to prevent this my mission; they would even talk to each other behind my back and say: 'Why does this fellow throw himself into danger among enemies who have no knowledge of God?' It was not malice, but it did not appeal to them because – and to this I own myself – of my rusticity. And I did not realize at once the grace that was then in me; now I understand that I should have done so before.

Now I have given a simple account to my brethren and fellow servants who have believed me because of what I said and still say in order to strengthen and confirm your faith. Would that you, too, would strive for greater things and do better! This will be my glory, for a wise son is the glory of his father.

You know, and so does God, how I have lived among you from my youth in the true faith and in sincerity of heart. Likewise, as regards the heathen among whom I live, I have been faithful to them, and so I shall be. God knows it, I have overreached none of them, nor would I think of doing so, for the sake of God and His Church, for fear of raising persecution against them and all of us, and for fear that through me the name of the Lord be blasphemed; for it is written: Woe to the man through whom the name of the Lord is blasphemed.

For although I be rude in all things, nevertheless I have tried somehow to keep myself safe, and that, too, for my Christian brethren, and the virgins of Christ, and the pious women who of their own accord made me gifts and laid on the altar some of their ornaments; and I gave them back to them, and they were offended that I did so. But I did it for the hope of lasting success – in order to preserve myself cautiously in everything so that they might not seize upon me or the ministry of my service, under the pretext of dishonesty, and that I would not even in the smallest matter give the infidels an opportunity to defame or defile.

When I baptized so many thousands of people, did I perhaps expect from any of them as much as half a scruple? Tell me, and I will restore it to you. Or when the Lord ordained clerics everywhere through my unworthy person and I conferred the ministry upon them free, if I asked any of them as much as the price of my shoes, speak against me and I will return it to you.

On the contrary, I spent money for you that they might receive me; and I went to you and everywhere for your sake in many dangers, even to the farthest districts, beyond which there lived nobody and where nobody had ever come to baptize, or to ordain clergy, or to confirm the people. With the grace of the Lord, I did everything lovingly and gladly for your salvation.

All the while I used to give presents to the kings, besides the fees I paid to their sons who travel with me. Even so they laid hands on me and my companions, and on that day they eagerly wished to kill me; but my time had not yet come. And everything they found with us they took away, and me they put in irons; and on the fourteenth day the Lord delivered me from their power, and our belongings were returned to us because of God and our dear friends whom we had seen before.

You know how much I paid to those who administered justice in all those districts to which I came frequently. I think I distributed among them not less than the price of fifteen men, so that you might enjoy me, and I might always enjoy you in God. I am not sorry for it – indeed it is not enough for me; I still spend and shall spend more. God has power to grant me afterwards that I myself may be spent for your souls.

Indeed, I call God to witness upon my soul that I lie not; neither, I hope, am I writing to you in order to make this an occasion of flattery or covetousness, nor because I look for honour from any of you. Sufficient is the honour that is not yet seen but is anticipated in the heart. Faithful is He that promised; He never lieth.

But I see myself exalted even in the present world beyond measure by the Lord, and I was not worthy nor such that He should grant me this. I know perfectly well, though not by my own judgement, that poverty and misfortune becomes me better than riches and pleasures. For Christ the Lord, too, was poor for our sakes; and I, unhappy wretch that I am, have no wealth even if I wished for it. Daily I expect murder, fraud, or capitivity, or whatever it may be; but I fear none of these things because of the promises of heaven. I have cast myself into the hands of God Almighty, who rules everywhere, as the prophet says: Cast thy thought upon God, and He shall sustain thee.

So, now I commend my soul to my faithful God, for whom I am an ambassador in all my wretchedness; but God accepteth no person, and chose me for this office – to be, although among His least, one of His ministers.

Hence let me render unto Him for all He has done to me. But what can I say or what can I promise to my Lord, as I can do nothing that He has not given me? May He search the hearts and deepest feelings; for greatly and exceedingly do I wish, and ready I was, that He should give me His chalice to drink, as He gave it also to the others who loved Him.

Wherefore may God never permit it to happen to me that I should lose His people which He purchased in the utmost parts of the world. I pray to God to give me perseverance and to deign that I be a faithful witness to Him to the end of my life for my God.

And if ever I have done any good for my God whom I love, I beg Him to grant me that I may shed my blood with those exiles and captives for His name, even though I should be denied a grave, or my body be woefully torn to pieces limb by limb by hounds or wild beasts, or the fowls of the air devour it. I am firmly convinced that if this should happen to me, I would have gained my soul together with my body, because on that day without doubt we shall rise in the brightness of the sun, that is, in the glory of Christ Jesus our Redeeemer, as sons of the living God and joint heirs with Christ, to be made conformable to His image; for of Him, and by Him, and in Him we shall reign.

For this sun which we see rises daily for us because He commands so, but it will never reign, nor will its splendour last; what is more, those wretches who adore it will be miserably punished. Not so we, who believe in, and worship, the true sun – Christ – who will never perish, nor will he who doeth His will; but he will abide for ever as Christ abideth for ever, who reigns with God the Father Almighty and the Holy Spirit before time, and now, and in all eternity. Amen.

Behold, again and again would I set forth the words of my confession. I testify in truth and in joy of heart before God and His holy angels that I never had any reason except the Gospel and its promises why I should ever return to the people from whom once before I barely escaped.

I pray those who believe and fear God, whosoever deigns to look at or receive this writing which Patrick, a sinner, unlearned, has composed in Ireland, that no one should ever say that it was my ignorance if I did or showed forth anything however small according to God's good pleasure; but let this be your conclusion and let it so be thought, that – as is the perfect truth – it was the gift of God. This is my confession before I die.

LETTER TO COROTICUS

I, Patrick, a sinner, unlearned, resident in Ireland, declare myself to be a bishop. Most assuredly I believe that what I am I have received from God. And so I live among barbarians, a stranger and exile for the love of God. He is witness that this is so. Not that I wished my mouth to utter anything so hard and harsh; but I am forced by the zeal for God; and the truth of Christ has wrung it from me, out of love for my neighbours and sons for whom I gave up my country and parents and my life to the point of death. If I be worthy, I live for my God to teach the heathen, even though some may despise me.

With my own hand I have written and composed these words, to be given, delivered, and sent to the soldiers of Coroticus; I do not say, to my fellow citizens, or to fellow citizens of the holy Romans, but to fellow citizens of the demons, because of their evil works. Like our enemies, they live in death, allies of the Scots and the apostate Picts. Dripping with blood, they welter in the blood of innocent Christians, whom I have begotten into the number for God and confirmed in Christ!

The day after the newly baptized, anointed with chrism, in white garments (had been slain) – the fragrance was still on their foreheads when they were butchered and slaughtered with the sword by the above-mentioned people – I sent a letter with a holy presbyter whom I had taught from his childhood, clerics accompanying him, asking them to let us have some of the booty, and of the baptized they had made captives. They only jeered at them.

Hence I do not know what to lament more: those who have been slain, or those whom they have taken captive, or those whom the devil has mightily ensnared. Together with him they will be slaves in Hell in an eternal punishment; for who committeth sin is a slave and will be called a son of the devil.

Wherefore let every God-fearing man know that they are enemies of me and of Christ my God, for whom I am an ambassador. Parricide! fratricide! ravening wolves that eat the people of the Lord as they eat bread! As is said, the wicked, O Lord, have destroyed Thy law, which but recently He had excellently and kindly planted in Ireland, and which had established itself by the grace of God.

I make no false claim. I share in the work of those whom He called and predestinated to preach the Gospel amidst grave persecutions unto the end of the earth, even if the enemy shows his jealousy through the tyranny of Coroticus, a man who has no respect for God nor for His priests whom He chose, giving them the highest, divine, and sublime power, that whom they should bind upon earth should be bound also in heaven.

Wherefore, then, I plead with you earnestly, ye holy and humble of heart, it is not permissible to court the favour of such people, nor to take food or drink with them, nor even to accept their alms, until they make reparation to God in hardships, through penance, with shedding of tears, and set free the baptized servants of God and handmaids of Christ, for whom He died and was crucified.

The most High disapproveth the gifts of the wicked . . . He that offereth sacrifice of the goods of the poor, is as one that sacrificeth the son in the presence of his father. The riches, it is written, which he has gathered unjustly, shall be vomited up from his belly; the angel of death drags him away, by the fury of dragons he shall be tormented, the viper's tongue shall kill him, unquenchable fire devoureth him. And so – Woe to those who fill themselves with what is not their own; or, What doth it profit a man that he gain the whole world, and suffer the loss of his own soul?

It would be too tedious to discuss and set forth everything in detail, to gather from the whole Law testimonies against such greed. Avarice is a deadly sin. Thou shalt not covet thy neighbour's goods. Thou shalt not kill. A murderer cannot be with Christ. Whosoever hateth his brother is accounted a murderer. Or, he that loveth not his brother abideth in death. How much more guilty is he that has stained his hands with blood of the sons of God whom He has of late purchased in the utmost part of the earth through the call of our littleness!

Did I come to Ireland without God, or according to the flesh? Who compelled me? I am bound by the Spirit not to see any of my kinsfolk. Is it of my own doing that I have holy mercy on the people who once took me captive and made away with the servants and maids of my father's house? I was freeborn according to the flesh. I am the son of a decurion. But I sold my noble rank – I am neither ashamed nor sorry – for the good of others. Thus I am a servant in Christ to a foreign nation for the unspeakable glory of life everlasting which is in Christ Jesus our Lord.

And if my own people do not know me, a prophet has no honour in his own country. Perhaps we are not of the same fold and have not one and the same God as father, as is written: He that is not with me, is against me, and he that gathereth not with me, scattereth. It is not right that one destroyeth, another buildeth up. I seek not the things that are mine.

It is not my grace, but God who has given this solicitude into my heart, to be one of His hunters or fishers whom God once foretold would come in the last days.

I am hated. What shall I do, Lord? I am most despised. Look, Thy sheep around me are torn to pieces and driven away, and that by those robbers, by the orders of the hostile-minded Coroticus. Far from the love of God is a man who hands over Christians to the Picts and Scots. Ravening wolves have devoured the flock of the Lord, which in Ireland was indeed growing splendidly with the greatest care; and the sons and daughters of kings were monks and virgins of Christ – I cannot count their number. Wherefore, be not pleased with the wrong done to the just; even to hell it shall not please.

Who of the saints would not shudder to be merry with such persons or to enjoy a meal with them? They have filled their houses with the spoils of dead Christians, they live on plunder. They do not know, the wretches, that what they offer their friends and sons as food is deadly poison, just as Eve did not understand that it was death she gave to her husband. So are all that do evil: they work death as their eternal punishment.

This is the custom of the Roman Christians of Gaul: they send holy and able men to the Franks and other heathen with so many thousand *solidi* to ransom baptized captives. You prefer to kill and sell them to a foreign nation that has no knowledge of God. You betray the members of Christ as it were into a brothel. What hope have you in God, or anyone who thinks as you do, or converses with you in words of flattery? God will judge. For Scripture says: Not only they that do evil are worthy to be condemned, but they also that consent to them.

I do not know what I should say or speak further about the departed ones of the sons of God, whom the sword has touched all too harshly. For Scripture says: Weep with them that weep; and again: If one member be grieved, let all members grieve with it. Hence the Church mourns and laments her sons and daughters whom the sword has not yet slain, but who were removed and carried off to faraway lands, where sin abounds openly, grossly, impudently. There people who were freeborn have been sold, Christians made slaves, and that, too, in the service of the abominable, wicked, and apostate Picts!

Therefore I shall raise my voice in sadness and grief: O you fair and beloved brethren and sons whom I have begotten in Christ, countless of number, what can I do you for? I am not worthy to come to the help of God or men. The wickedness of the wicked hath prevailed over us. We have been made, as it were, strangers. Perhaps they do not believe that we have received one and the same baptism, or have one and the same God as father. For them it is a disgrace that we are Irish. Have ye not, as is written, one God? Have ye, every one of you, forsaken his neighbour?

Therefore I grieve for you, I grieve, my dearly beloved. But again, I rejoice within myself. I have not laboured for nothing, and my journeying abroad has not been in vain. And if this horrible, unspeakable crime did happen – thanks be to God, you have left the world and have gone to Paradise as baptized faithful. I see you: you have begun to journey where night shall be no more, nor mourning, nor death; but you shall leap like calves loosened from their bonds, and you shall tread down the wicked, and they shall be ashes under your feet.

You, then, will reign with the apostles, and prophets, and martyrs. You will take possession of eternal kingdoms, as He Himself testifies, saying: They shall come from the east and from the west, and shall sit down with Abraham, and Isaac, and Jacob in the kingdom of heaven. Without are dogs, and sorcerers, . . . and murderers; and liars and perjurers have their portion in the pool of everlasting fire. Not without reason does the Apostle say: Where the just man shall scarcely be saved, where shall the sinner and ungodly transgressor of the law find himself?

Where, then, will Coroticus with his criminals, rebels against Christ, where will they see themselves, they who distribute baptized women as prizes – for a miserable temporal kingdom, which will pass away in a moment? As a cloud or smoke that is dispersed by the wind, so shall the deceitful wicked perish at the presence of the Lord; but the just shall feast with great constancy with Christ, they shall judge nations, and rule over wicked kings for ever and ever. Amen.

I testify before God and His angels that it will be so as He indicated to my ignorance. It is not my words that I have set forth in Latin, but those of God and the apostles and prophets, who have never lied. He that believeth shall be saved; but he that believeth not shall be condemned, God hath spoken.

I ask earnestly that whoever is a willing servant of God be a carrier of this letter, so that on no account it be suppressed or hidden by anyone, but rather be read before all the people, and in the presence of Coroticus himself. May God inspire them sometime to recover their senses for God, repenting, however late, their heinous deeds – murderers of the brethren of the Lord! – and to set free the baptized women whom they took captive, in order that they may deserve to live to God, and be made whole, here and in eternity! Be peace to the Father, and to the Son, and to the Holy Spirit. Amen.

(Translated by Ludwig Bieler)

APPENDIX II
Muirchú's Miracles

1. NEWLY BAPTIZED VIRGIN MEETS HER MAKER
Monesan, the daughter of a British King, at a time when Britain was still pagan, refused to marry in spite of beatings and soakings with cold water. She sought the true God. Her parents heard of Patrick, 'a just man [who] was visited by eternal God every seventh day', so they took their daughter to Ireland and after much effort met him. Patrick asked her if she believed in God. She said yes, he baptized her and she immediately dropped dead. Her relics are now worshipped.

2. COROTICUS CHANGES INTO A FOX
This is the only mention of Coroticus in Muirchú. Coroticus was a cruel ruler and persecutor of Christians. Patrick chastised him by means of a letter but Coroticus scorned his words. When Patrick heard that, he prayed to God asking him to 'expel this godless man from this world and from the next'. Coroticus, in the middle of a public place and before the eyes of his followers 'was ignominiously changed into a fox, went off, and since that day and hour, like water that flows away, was never seen again.'

3. BENIGNUS PRAYING IN THE RIVER
Young Benignus has already been established as a favourite among Patrick's disciples. Patrick discovered that the holy boy shared his ability to have visions of heaven and appointed him his successor. They went together to pray in the middle of the river bed. Benignus admitted he could not stand the cold water, so Patrick sent him to the lower river. Here poor Benignus soon found the water too hot and went on land.

4. MACC CUIL GOES TO THE ISLE OF MAN
Macc Cuil moccu Greccae was a wicked godless ruler who ambushed travellers and killed them. One day Patrick came his way. Macc Cuill knew of his reputation as a wonder-worker and decided to set a trap for him. He made one of his band lie down and pretend to be mortally ill. When Patrick approached he was asked to heal the man. Patrick knew what they were up to and said, 'It would not be strange if he had been ill.' When his companions uncovered the man's face they found he was dead. The robber band repented and were converted.

177

Macc Cuil confessed he had planned to kill Patrick and asked for further penance. Patrick told him to take no property except one short garment, to fetter his feet with an iron chain, throw its key into the sea, get into a small boat without rudder or oar, let the sea take him where it will, and practise the commandments for the rest of his life wherever he landed. Macc Cuil agreed, and asked what they should do about the dead man. Patrick brought him back to life. Macc Cuil set off as instructed and landed on the Isle of Man, whose two bishops took pity on him, and where he now lives as their successor.

5. KEEP HOLY THE SABBATH
Patrick's day of rest was disturbed by some pagans digging the moat of a *rath*. He forbade them to work on a Sunday but they laughed at him. Patrick cursed them saying, 'in spite of all your labour you shall achieve nothing' and just as he predicted, the next night there was a storm that destroyed all their work.

6. GRAZACHAM OR THE FOUNDING OF ARMAGH
Patrick asked a wealthy and honoured man, Dáire, to give him a certain hill in Armagh. Dáire did not want to give that hill away, but gave Patrick another lower down. Dáire then sent a horse to graze on Patrick's land. Patrick was offended by a brute animal disturbing the small place dedicated to God. The horse died the next day, and Dáire ordered his men to go and kill Patrick. At that moment Dáire was struck down dead and his wife countermanded his order. Two men went to Patrick and told him only that Dáire had been taken ill. Patrick knew what they had in mind, so he gave them holy water and told them to sprinkle it over their [dead] horse and take the horse away. The horse revived. They sprinkled the water over Dáire and he too came back to life. Dáire decided to give Patrick a magnificent bronze cauldron as a token of honour. On receiving the gift Patrick merely said 'Grazacham' (a corruption of *gratias agamus* – 'let us give thanks'). When Dáire got home he decided Patrick was a fool to say nothing but 'grazacham' for such a great gift, so he ordered his servants to fetch it back. When they told Patrick what they wanted he said 'Grazacham, take it.' When Dáire heard this he was so impressed with Patrick's 'Grazachams' that he went in person to return the vessel, praising Patrick for his steadfastness. He also gave him the piece of land that Patrick had asked for in the first place, and this is the city which is now called Armagh.

I will let Muirchú conclude this miracle in his own words, as it is the only occasion on which he adds a humanizing touch to the legend:

And they went out together, holy Patrick and Dáire, to inspect the marvellous and pleasing gift that he had offered, and they climbed to the top of that hill and found there a doe with its little fawn lying in the place where there is now the altar of the northern church at Armagh, and the companions of Patrick wanted to catch the fawn and kill it, but the holy man objected and forbade them to do so. He even took up the fawn himself and carried it on his shoulders, and the doe followed him like a meek and loving lamb until he let the fawn go in another glen, to the north of Armagh, where, as knowledgeable men tell us, there persist to the present day signs of his miraculous power.

7. GREEDY MAN PUNISHED
A greedy man refused to let Patrick's oxen rest and graze in his field. Patrick was angry and cursed the field saying that henceforth it would be useless. That very same day the field was flooded by the sea and it has remained sandy and barren ever since.

8. THE MISPLACED CROSS
Every time Patrick saw a cross on his journeys he used to get out of his chariot and pray there. One day he missed one and when they reached the inn which was their destination the charioteer commented on this. Patrick left the inn and retraced his steps and prayed before the cross. He asked the dead man in the tomb who he was. The dead man answered that he was a pagan buried near a Christian. The Christian's mother, in her distress, had put the cross on the wrong tomb. 'That explains why I did not see it,' said Patrick, and the cross was moved to the correct place.

9. DRY FIELD IN A STORM
Patrick's custom was never to travel between Saturday night and Monday morning. One very rainy Sunday he was spending the night in a field and though 'heavy rain raged in the whole country' Patrick's field stayed dry.

10. A LIGHT FOR LOST HORSES
Patrick's charioteer was very distressed because he had lost his horses and could not search for them in the dark. Patrick raised his hand and his five fingers lit up like lights. The charioteer found his horses. (Muirchú adds that the charioteer kept this miracle secret until Patrick's death.)

11. PATRICK'S FOUR REQUESTS
As death was approaching Patrick asked to be taken to Armagh. On his way he saw a burning bush in which the Angel Victor appeared and told him that if he retraced his steps to Saul his four requests would be granted. The requests were:
    a) that Patrick's pre-eminence shall be in Armagh;
    b) that whoever recites Patrick's hymn on the day of his death will be judged by Patrick as regards penance;
    c) that Dichu's descendants will find mercy and not perish;
    d) that all the Irish will be judged by Patrick on the Day of Judgement.
    Victor told Patrick to go back and die in Saul, and Muirchú adds that this happened on 17 March when Patrick was 120 years old.

12. LIGHTNESS AT THE HOUR OF DEATH

On the day of Patrick's death there was no night, nor did night fall in the province for twelve days after.

13. ST PATRICK'S WAKE

During the first night of Patrick's wake angels kept vigil and the men slept. During the other nights, men kept vigil, but the angels left a sweet smell behind them.

14. UNTAMED OXEN CHOOSE BURIAL PLACE

Before his death the angel advised Patrick to have two untamed oxen yoked to the cart carrying his body and let them lead him to his burial place. They chose Dun Lethglaisse (Downpatrick).

15. FIRE BURST FROM THE TOMB

When Patrick's tomb was disturbed by men building a church above it fire burst forth from it.

16. WAR OVER RELICS AVERTED

There was bitter contention for Patrick's relics between the Uí Neill and the Ulaid. To prevent the shedding of blood the wild sea rose up between the two tribes and stopped their people from fighting.

NOTES

For general historical background I have relied mainly on the 12-volume Gill & Macmillan *History of Ireland* (Dublin, 1972–6) together with:
    T. W. Moody and F. X. Martin (ed.), *The Course of Irish History* (Dublin, rev. edn 1984)
    Kenneth Neill, *An Illustrated History of the Irish People* (Dublin, 1979)
    Lord Killanin and Michael V. Duignan, *The Shell Guide to Ireland* (Dublin, rev. edn 1969)

CHAPTER ONE: *EGO PATRICIUS*

General sources for early Irish History:
    J. F. Kenney, *Sources for the Early History of Ireland 1. Ecclesiastical* (New York, 1929)
    Gearóid MacNiocaill, *Ireland Before the Vikings*, (Dublin, 1972)
All quotations from the *Confession* and the *Letter to Coroticus* are from the translation by Ludwig Bieler (see Appendix I).
For interpretation and explanation of Saint Patrick's writings, I have evolved my own synthesis of material in:
    Ludwig Bieler, *The Life and Legend of Saint Patrick*
    Eóin MacNeill, *Saint Patrick, Apostle of Ireland*
    R. P. C. Hanson, *The Life and Writings of the Historical Saint Patrick*

CHAPTER TWO: THE EARLIEST *LIVES* AND THE LECALE PENINSULA

My accounts of Muirchú and Tirechán are based on the relevant volumes in the Early Irish Texts series, translated and annotated by Ludwig Bieler.
1 This was pointed out to me by Charles Doherty of University College, Dublin, author of *Early Medieval Ireland* (Dublin, 1988)
2 Robin Flower, in *The Irish Tradition* (Oxford, 1947)
3 D. A. Binchy, 'Saint Patrick and his Biographers Ancient and Modern', in *Studia Hibernica* (1962)
4 The change in the nature of Saint Patrick's spirituality was brought to my attention by A. J. R. Harvey, Editorial Secretary of the *Dictionary of Medieval Latin from Celtic Sources* at the Royal Irish Academy.

5 Robert Lloyd Praeger, *Official Guide to Co. Down and the Mourne Mountains* (Belfast, 1898)

CHAPTER THREE: THE *TRIPARTITE LIFE* AND CROAGHPATRICK

I used Whitley Stoke's edition of the *Tripartite Life* (Rolls Series, 1887).
For the history of Croaghpatrick I used *The Life and Writings of Saint Patrick* by the Revd Dr Healey, Archbishop of Tuam (Dublin, 1905); the pamphlet *Croaghpatrick* by F. P. Carey (Irish Messenger Publications, 1955); and the *Shell Guide*.

CHAPTER FOUR: THE NORMAN VIEW AND DOWNPATRICK

All Giraldus quotations are from Gerald of Wales, *The History and Topography of Ireland*, trans. John J. O'Meara (Harmondsworth, 1982).
All Jocelin quotations are from *The Life and Acts of Saint Patrick*, trans. Edmund L. Swift (Dublin, 1809).

CHAPTER FIVE: SAINT PATRICK'S PURGATORY: LOUGH DERG

My major source for this chapter was Shane Leslie's compilation of documents *Saint Patrick's Purgatory* (London, 1932). Accounts of early pilgrims are given in his translation.
I also used *Lough Derg* by Alice Curtayne, especially for its chronology, and read Henry of Saltrey in *Saint Patrick's Purgatory* (Dublin, 1985), trans. Jean Michel Picard, introduction by Bishop Duffy. Also useful, for its brevity and clarity, was *Lough Derg* by Lawrence J. Flynn – the same Father Flynn to whom I talked on the island; it has excellent colour illustrations.

CHAPTER SIX: THE GREENING OF SAINT PATRICK

Additional information on sorrel and scurvy grass from Roger Phillips, *Wild Food* (London, 1983).
Patrick J. Corish, *The Catholic Community in the Seventeenth and Eighteenth Centuries* (Dublin, 1981) provided me with much material for the latter part of this chapter, including the extract from *The Good Confessor*.

CHAPTER SEVEN: SAINT PATRICK'S DAY

1 The figure of 15 million cards was quoted by Hallmark Cards to John J. Concannon, co-author of *The Irish Directory* (New York, 1983).
2 Statistics in this chapter on emigration and the social classification of emigrants are taken from D. Fitzpatrick, *Irish Emigration 1801–1921* (Dublin, 1984).
3 Details of early Saint Patrick's Day celebrations are taken from

contemporary records published in John D. Crimmins, *Saint Patrick's Day: Its Celebration in New York and other American Places 1737–1845* (New York, 1902).

4 The relationship between the Civil War, Irish identity and Saint Patrick's Day parades was pointed out to me by Kevin T. McEneaney of the American Irish Historical Society.

5 John J. Concannon, historian of the New York County and New York State AOH. His remarks are published in the *Irish Directory*.

CHAPTER EIGHT: ALTHOUGH IT IS THE NIGHT

Statistics on the frequency of academic works on Saint Patrick were extracted from material which will eventually appear as the definitive bibliography of Patrician studies. This was kindly made available to me by A. J. R. Harvey (see ch. 2, n. 4).

My mentor to the complexities of nineteenth- and twentieth-century Patrician studies has been Ludwig Bieler's excellent study *The Life and Legend of Saint Patrick*. His division of scholars into 'rational' and 'pre-critical' is adopted in this chapter. D. A. Binchy's long article 'Saint Patrick and his Biographers Ancient and Modern' was also very useful.

The historian Brian Murphy (of Glenstal Abbey at the time of writing) provided me with invaluable references on the connections between Patrician studies and the Gaelic League.

Father Patrick D. Dundon of the Irish Missionary Union provided the statistics on Irish missions quoted in this chapter and several very helpful references.

1 James Plunket, *The Gems She Wore* (London, 1972).

2 Hanson, *The Life and Writings of the Historical Saint Patrick*.

3 From *Station Island*, Section IX, by Seamus Heaney (London, 1984). Ironically, and not insignificantly (true spirituality knows no borders), these lines are a translation of the poem 'Cantar del alma que se huelga de conoscer a Dios por fé' by Saint John of the Cross.

SUGGESTIONS FOR FURTHER READING

The most up-to-date general work on Saint Patrick and early Irish history is Volume One of the Helicon History of Ireland: *Early Medieval Ireland* by Charles Doherty (Dublin, 1988). The author stresses the importance of the Gaulish settlements in Ireland before and after Saint Patrick's time, using new archaeological evidence.

Probably the closest to a standard twentieth-century life of Saint Patrick is *Saint Patrick Apostle of Ireland* by Eóin MacNeill (Dublin, 1934 and many reprints). This short work combines erudition and original historical research with readability; although many of its conclusions have been overtaken by subsequent research it remains an excellent introduction.

The Life and Writings of the Historical Saint Patrick by R. P. C. Hanson (New York, 1983) emphasizes Saint Patrick's identity as a Roman Briton. After a detailed introduction, Hanson, historian, theologian and classical scholar, guides the reader through Saint Patrick's own writings paragraph by paragraph, explaining when and how controversies have arisen and, by close attention to the language, casting much interesting light on the texts.

The best starting point for anyone interested in the history of Patrician studies is *The Life and Legend of Saint Patrick* by Ludwig Bieler (Dublin and London, 1949). Bieler, palaeographer and Latin scholar, dedicated much of his life to the study of texts associated with Saint Patrick and is responsible for the standard editions of most of them. Much of his work is necessarily of a highly technical nature, but this short book is an exception. His enthusiasm for the scholars who have dedicated themselves to the study of Saint Patrick is infectious, and his bibliography and notes constitute the perfect introduction to a fascinating phase of intellectual history.

Saint Patrick ed. Revd John Ryan (Dublin, 1958) contains a series of radio lectures given by leading scholars when the controversies over Saint Patrick's identity were at their height. Even though the arguments are often abstruse, they remain accessible and often surprisingly amusing.

Lough Derg by Alice Curtayne (Omagh, 1976), a detailed and conscientious work, is recognized as the standard history. A pithier history, with excellent colour illustrations, is *Lough Derg* by Lawrence J. Flynn (Dublin, 1986).

INDEX

PHOTO CREDITS

Mount Slemish *Courtesy of The Northern Ireland Tourist Board, Belfast (NITB)*
Statue at Slieve Patrick *NITB*
Struell Wells *NITB*
Saul Church *NITB*
Souvenir stall at Murrisk © *The Irish Times*
Pilgrim on Croaghpatrick with ash plant © *The Irish Times*
Line of Pilgrims on Croaghpatrick © *Liam Lyons*
Remains of Inch Abbey *NITB*
Saint Patrick's 'gravestone' *NITB*
Aerial view of Station Island © *Bord Failte, Dublin*
17th-century map of Lough Derg *Courtesy of Jarrolds Publications, Norwich, reproduced by permission of the National Library of Ireland*
The Basilica of Saint Patrick *Courtesy of Jarrolds Publications, Norwich*
Present-day pilgrims on Station Island © *Edward Winters and by kind permission of Mgr McSorley, St Patrick's Purgatory*
19th-century pilgrims © *Edward Winters/ St Patrick's Purgatory*

Pilgrims returning to the mainland *Courtesy of Jarrolds Publications, Norwich*
Betelius' map of Ireland, *c.* 1590 *British Library*
Botanical drawings of the shamrock *Courtesy of The Royal Botanic Gardens, Kew*
Aer Lingus logo © *Aer Lingus*
Iron bell and shrine *Courtesy of The National Museum of Ireland*
Two images of Saint Patrick (contrasting with Thomas Messingham's engraving) *Mary Evans Picture Library*
Limestone carving of Saint Patrick from Faughart *Courtesy of the National Museum of Ireland*
Stained-glass window from St Mary's Church, Thame *Sonia Halliday*
Stained-glass window by Harry Clarke *Courtesy of 'Ireland of the Welcomes' Magazine*
Saint Patrick's Day parade in Dublin © *The Irish Press*
Saint Patrick's Day parade in New York © *The Irish Echo, NY*